Kiddiwalks

IN THE
PEAK DISTRICT

◇◇◇◇◇◇◇◇◇◇◇◇◇◇◇◇◇◇◇◇◇◇◇◇◇◇◇◇◇◇◇

John & Anne Nuttall

COUNTRYSIDE BOOKS
NEWBURY BERKSHIRE

First published 2009
© John & Anne Nuttall 2009

All rights reserved. No reproduction
permitted without the prior permission
of the publisher:

COUNTRYSIDE BOOKS
3 Catherine Road
Newbury, Berkshire

To view our complete range of books,
please visit us at
www.countrysidebooks.co.uk

ISBN 978 1 84674 136 4

*For Heather, Elizabeth, Samuel,
John, Beatrice and Matthew*

Photographs by John Nuttall

Produced through MRM Associates Ltd., Reading
Typeset by Jean Cussons Typesetting, Diss, Norfolk
Printed by Information Press, Oxford

Contents

AREA MAP SHOWING LOCATION OF THE WALKS

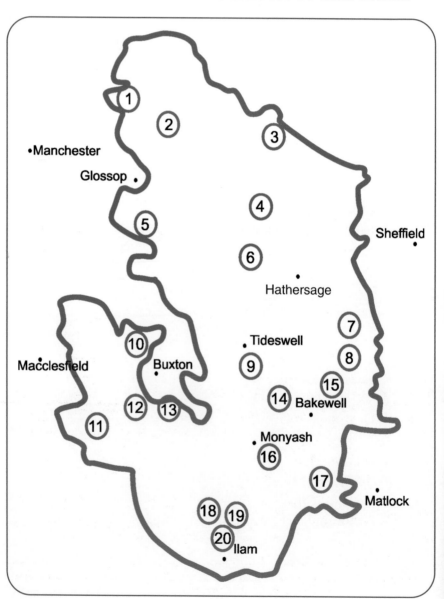

Contents

PUBLISHER'S NOTE

We hope that you obtain considerable enjoyment from this book; great care has been taken in its preparation. Although at the time of publication all routes followed public rights of way or permitted paths, diversion orders can be made and permissions withdrawn.

We cannot, of course, be held responsible for such diversion orders and any inaccuracies in the text which result from these or any other changes to the routes nor any damage which might result from walkers trespassing on private property. We are anxious though that all details covering the walks are kept up to date and would therefore welcome information from readers which would be relevant to future editions.

The simple sketch maps that accompany the walks in this book are based on notes made by the author whilst checking out the routes on the ground. They are designed to show you how to reach the start, to point out the main features of the overall circuit and they contain a progression of numbers that relate to the paragraphs of the text.

However, for the benefit of a proper map, we do recommend that you purchase the relevant Ordnance Survey sheet covering your walk. The Ordnance Survey maps are widely available, especially through booksellers and local newsagents.

Introduction

Keeping children happy is all a matter of planning interesting outings and making them enjoyable. These days youngsters are so cosseted and protected that sometimes the fun gets taken out of going for a walk. Balancing along a wall is a lot better than walking beside it, while tiptoeing across stepping stones or paddling through a stream is much more exciting than crossing the bridge. Yes, it's a bit hazardous, someone might get dirty or fall over, but it also brings a lot more enjoyment. So next time, maybe it'll be the children who say 'Can we please go for a walk?'

The Peak District was the first of all the National Parks to be created and its variety of walking is unsurpassed. From the wild country of the eastern moors to flower-filled limestone dales, the Peak District has it all. Cressbrook Dale never ceases to amaze with its variety of flowers, while the cowslips of Taddington are dazzling. And adventure is there in plenty. Thor's Cave has the biggest entrance in England, the chasm of Lud's Church has a slightly scary allure, while Lathkill Dale combines flowers with the tunnels of a bygone mining industry. People flock to the stately mansion of Chatsworth, but the woods at the back are silent and mysterious, while the Goyt Valley boasts a ruined mansion set amid thousands of rhododendrons. There are expanses of open water at Torside Reservoir and Langsett, while Dovestone Reservoir is completely encircled by a pushchair route. Baslow Edge has rock climbers to watch, and after climbing Higger Tor and the ancient hill fort of Carl Wark you can paddle in the stream beneath a packhorse bridge. There's more paddling too at Three Shires Head, where forgers once escaped the police by crossing the packhorse bridge to another county. Children can dance in the stone circle on Stanton Moor and at Solomon's Temple there's a tower with a spiral staircase to climb. The little village of Ilam has a river boiling out of the ground, while Dove Dale has both a summit and stepping stones. For anyone who thinks the best walks go to a summit, Crook Hill makes a fine objective and so does Lantern Pike, but, while Mam Tor certainly has a summit, children will be fascinated by the cataclysmic collapse of the road.

Solomon's Temple, Grin Low.

When our sons were young we took them walking. Fields and hills, moors and mountains were their playgrounds, while a papoose carrier was a vital piece of equipment. Now we have six grandchildren; they all love the outdoors and our happiest days are the ones we spend walking with them. They have been very patient models for this book and having them all to ourselves for the day is especially rewarding. We hope you enjoy the walks as much as we did, for walking with children is fun!

John and Anne Nuttall
www.nuttalls.com

1

Dovestone Reservoir

A Watery Stroll

Alphin and his friend Alderman were giants who lived opposite each other on the hillsides above the deep and beautiful valley now filled by Dovestone Reservoir. One day Alphin quarrelled with Alderman over a nymph, named Rimmon, who lived in Chew Brook and soon they started to throw stones at each other. Massive boulders flew back and forth, crashing into the hillsides and the air was rent with their roars of rage. Alas, eventually poor Alphin was killed, but it must have been a big battle, for you can still see the results of their quarrel in the piles of boulders lying on the hillside. Some people say this is nonsense, the boulders are all due to erosion and the Ice Age, but lots of places have erosion, only Dovestone Reservoir has giants.

Dovestone Reservoir

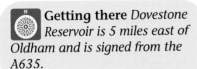 **Getting there** *Dovestone Reservoir is 5 miles east of Oldham and is signed from the A635.*

Length of walk 2½ miles (or 4 miles if you continue around Yeoman Hey reservoir).
Time Up to 2 hours.
Terrain The Dovestone Reservoir Circuit has surfaced paths, suitable for pushchairs. The walk can be extended to 4 miles by looping round Yeoman Hey Reservoir, but this would not be suitable for pushchairs.
Start/Parking Dovestone Reservoir car park, small charge (GR 013036). There are toilets and even a tap to clean your boots.
Map OS Explorer OL1 – Dark Peak area.

Refreshments There will probably be a refreshment van, but the walk passes Ashway Gap, a lovely place for a picnic.

❶ From the top end of Dovestone Reservoir car park continue along the track to an information board and on past the sailing club. High up on the right lie Wimberry Stones, (wimberry is the local name for bilberries) while on the far side of the reservoir rises Alderman's Hill. You pass an enclosure of sailing boats. How many are there? You can also count the boats on the reservoir. Next you go by the memorial forest 'Life for a Life'.

❷ The track crosses Chew Brook, an ideal paddling spot, then you fork left over the footbridge and

Fun Things to See and Do ◆

 As you set off, tell the children **the story of the two giants,** Alderman and Alphin.

There is a **permanent orienteering course,** suitable for pushchairs, but this has to be planned ahead, as map-packs must be purchased in advance from Brownhill Visitor Centre or Uppermill Tourist Information Centre. Children can look out for the red triangles marking the orienteering controls even if you don't have a map.

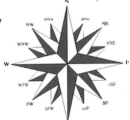

9 ◆

1

The Walk

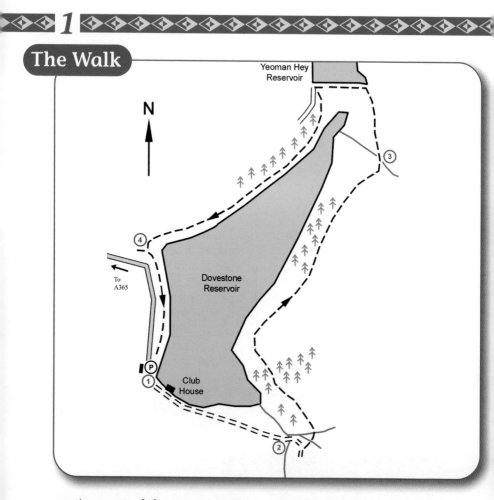

continue round the reservoir. The path goes below a quarry and past a wood to the picnic area on the site of Ashway Gap House. Here an information board tells you all about the now demolished Gothic house, home of the Platt family. There is a lovely view up to Dove Stone Rocks.

3 The track crosses a bridge,

then leads over Yeoman Hey Reservoir Dam, with Ashway Rocks high above. Continue along the track for a few yards; then turn left through the kissing gate and head downhill. Here the woodland is a splendid place for hide and seek. The path continues beside the reservoir and past a seat where, looking across the valley, you can see the spoil heaps and outflow of the Ashway Gap tunnel.

Chew Brook.

4 Reaching the dam you can look down on Fletchers Paper Mill and the back to back mill workers' cottages at Forty Row. After a short, steep slope downhill you cross the concrete spillway with its three tipping steel fusegates, built in 1995 to safeguard the dam in the event of a 1 in 100,000 year flood. Then the dam leads back to the car park.

Background Notes ◆

Set amid the encircling high Saddleworth Moors, **Dovestone Reservoir** is a surprisingly late newcomer to the scene, having been constructed in 1967. It is used primarily as compensation water but it can supply drinking water by pumping into Yeoman Hey Reservoir. It also supplies Fletchers Paper Mill, which produces very fine quality paper suitable for cigarette papers – and bibles. There is a sailing club.

The higher **Yeoman Hey Reservoir** was the cause of a lot of trouble. When, in 1880, the waters of the north-western moors were channelled into the newly built reservoir, the mill owners complained loudly – not only was the water board taking the water from their mills, they did not even own the moors from which it was flowing! The result of the dispute was a ¾-mile long tunnel which diverted the water so it bypassed Yeoman Hey Reservoir. The water now flows directly into Dovestone Reservoir. Though often dry, in flood conditions the **Ashway Gap tunnel** fills to the brim and an awesome amount of water gushes out of the far end.

Torside Reservoir

Railway and Reservoirs

W hen they built the long chain of reservoirs that stretch for over four miles up the Longdendale Valley, people were frightened. Holme Reservoir in Yorkshire had collapsed and the locals were fearful of living with this new threat. And this was no tentative approach, as the engineer John Bateman had designed the five reservoirs to be the longest stretch of man-made water in the world. Then along came the railway and this also was a world beater, for its twin tunnels were the longest ever. Well, they needn't have worried, the reservoirs are still here and at weekends Torside is busy with yachts tacking up and down or unfurling spinnakers for an extra turn of speed. But although they built a new tunnel as late as 1954, the days when the trains thundered up the valley and deep under the moors to Yorkshire have gone, and now the track is a way for walkers, cyclists, horses and even prams.

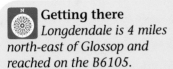

Getting there
Longdendale is 4 miles north-east of Glossop and reached on the B6105.

Length of walk 4 miles.
Time Allow about 3 hours.
Terrain Easy paths, but only the Longdendale Trail is suitable for pushchairs (see map).
Start/Parking Torside Information Centre on the B6105. Pay and display car park, toilets (GR 068983).
Map OS Explorer OL1 – Dark Peak area.

Refreshments No refreshments en route, but lots of handy seats for picnics. In the summer months, there may be an ice cream van.

1 Take the path from the top leftmost corner of Torside car park, leading up to the Longdendale Trail, part of the Trans Pennine Trail. This is a route for cyclists, horse riders and walkers stretching from Liverpool to Hull and on to Istanbul! Turn left along the surfaced track, which follows the route of the disused railway

◆ Fun Things to See and Do ◆

This walk is remarkably good for **flowers** so be sure and pack a flower book; then the children can help identify any you don't recognise. You will even find some lime-loving flowers among the gritstone where limestone chippings were dumped to make foundations for the railway.

The route is well signed and the children will enjoy looking out for the waymarks. In the pinewoods there are **cones to hunt for** and there may be **sailing boats** on the reservoir tacking to and fro.

Look out for **wildfowl** on the reservoir – binoculars would be useful. You may see teal, pochard, golden eye and tufted duck while in winter Beswick swans come here from Siberia.

past verges that are flower-filled for much of the year and through woodland and open glades.

2 When the Trail reaches the road you double back, signed 'Crowden'. Crossing the road, follow the track down through pine trees to Woodhead Reservoir dam. High above is Woodhead Chapel, in whose churchyard are the unmarked graves of many navvies and their families who died of cholera when building the second Woodhead Tunnel in 1849. Cross the walkway, then go

up a flight of steps and follow the raised embankment past a wildlife sanctuary beside a stone lined leat. You can glimpse the roof of Crowden Youth Hostel off to the right – the first overnight stop for many Pennine Way walkers.

3 Keep straight on, then turn left at the wooden kissing gate. The path leads down to Torside Reservoir edge and follows the route of the railway used to construct the reservoirs and then later for maintenance work, until the 1940s. Crossing

The Walk

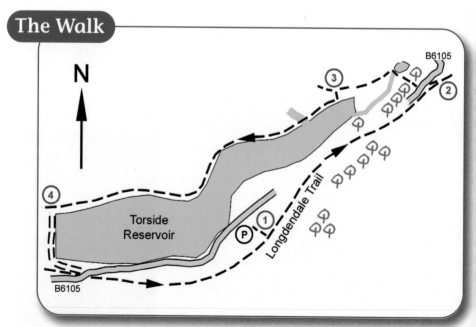

Crowden Brook.

Crowden Brook, you continue through the bracken; then, after passing the sailing club on the opposite bank, go over the wooden bridge and climb the steps. Beyond some fine beech trees the path joins the Pennine Way and continues through tall Scots pines, a good spot for hide and seek.

4 Reaching Torside dam go down the steps and cross the dam above Rhodeswood Reservoir. This was begun in 1849, destroying Rhode Mill, and took only three years to build, while Torside, started at the same time, took 20 years to complete. The broad track then leads gently uphill to the road, where you turn right for a few yards. Turn left along the Trail, where an information board tells the history of Longdendale. Up to the right lies the deep rift of Torside Clough, where the Pennine Way follows the valley rim. It isn't much further along the track and then you are back at Torside car park.

Kiddiwalks in the Peak District

◆ Background Notes ◆

From Woodhead in the east to Bottoms in the west, the **Longdendale reservoirs** were, at the time they were constructed, the longest expanse of artificial water in the world. Woodhead Reservoir, authorised by an Act of Parliament in 1846 permitting the damming of the River Etherow, was quickly followed by Torside Reservoir and Rhodeswood Reservoir. Valehouse Reservoir and Bottoms Reservoir came a little later and these are compensation reservoirs that store water to regulate the downstream flow of the River Etherow. The engineer responsible was the magnificently named John Frederic La Trobe Bateman, a bearded Victorian who encountered considerable difficulties and received a lot of opposition from the local mill owners, some of whom would lose their mills as they disappeared under water, while those downstream thought they would no longer have a water supply. No doubt he wasn't very popular either with the hamlets of Torside, Vale House and Bottoms, which were to be drowned.

The disused railway track of the Sheffield to Manchester Railway is now the **Longdendale Trail**, which leads from Hadfield for 6 miles to the Woodhead Tunnel. This was the route of the first rail link between Manchester and Sheffield, which opened in the 1840s and closed in 1981.

Langsett

Woodland and Water

In the woods.

Some rivers are nameless, while others are known worldwide, but it's unusual to find a river with two names, 'The Porter or Little Don'. Was there a competition to find the best name and was it a dead heat? Langsett, tucked away in the north-east corner of the Peak District National Park, is sometimes called Little Switzerland, but the valley reminds us more of the long glens reaching up into the Scottish Highlands. Tall pine trees stand by the river, while above are the moors, a magnificent country of boundless heather stretching for miles over the wild solitude of Bleaklow. But for all the wilderness beyond, the reservoir makes a good pushchair walk, not perfectly flat and requiring a bit of effort, but with a spot to picnic and paddle there's no need to hurry.

3

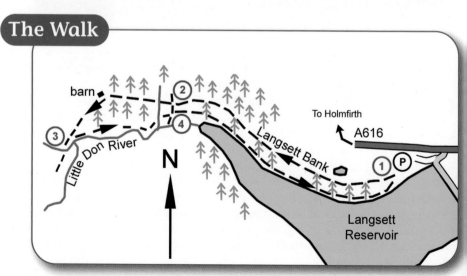

Getting there *Langsett Barn is 3 miles south-west of Penistone and signed from the A616.*

Length of walk Pushchair walk 2½ miles, longer walk 3½ miles.
Time Make this a half-day expedition.
Terrain Reasonable pushchair paths on the shorter walk. The longer walk has steps and the odd muddy patch.
Start/Parking Langsett Barn pay and display car park, toilets (GR 211004).
Map OS Explorer OL1 – Dark Peak area.
Refreshments The Waggon and Horses pub and the Bank View café in Langsett village.

1 From the far top corner of Langsett car park take the path between the walls, then fork right in the trees. This climbs gently along the edge of Langsett Bank, staying to the left of the wall and on through banks of bilberries. Where a path leads out to a pond in a heather covered old quarry, there is a good climbing tree. Keeping straight on, the track narrows past huge gritstone boulders. You have to bump the pushchair down a shallow flight of steps, then the path continues through the trees and dips across the end of a forest track.

2 Reaching a broad track, the *pushchair walk* turns downhill and continues at point 4. The *longer*

The Walk

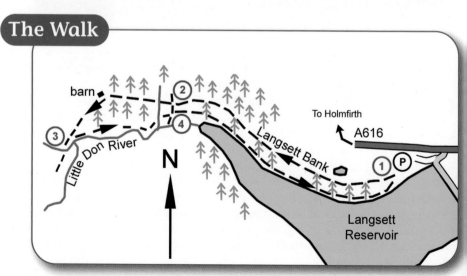

walk keeps straight on over the rightmost wooden bridge and through a forest glade, climbing gently uphill to Swinden, whose name recalls the pigs that once foraged here for acorns. The original Swinden Farm, inhabited until the 1950s, has been demolished. Follow the track round the back of the old barn; then go through the wooden gate. A path leads down through the

Background Notes

There are many more trees than people in Langsett and certainly far more grouse on **Langsett Moor**, whose three and a half thousand acres belong to Sir Thomas Pilkington and are managed for game.

Langsett has newly-built expensive cottages, a Gothic valve tower, a copy of a turret at Lancaster Castle and a beautiful old barn that was converted to a visitor centre, but closed, alas, when the government cut the grant to the National Park.

Langsett Reservoir, which was started in 1889 and completed in 1904, now belongs to Yorkshire Water. It supplies Rotherham and Doncaster, and, though access to the water's edge is forbidden, the lake adds to the beauty of the scene.

The **Porter or Little Don River**, which rises high on the Howden Moors, has cut down through the hillside, exposing bedding planes of alternate rock and shale. These are seen well just above Brookhouse Bridge, while upstream there are beautiful Scots pines, reminiscent of the lower slopes of the Cairngorms. Below the reservoir the acidic, peat-stained water is treated at the Langsett Treatment Works, built in the 1980s. Beyond Langsett Reservoir the river continues to join the River Don at Stocksbridge.

Brookhouse Farm was one of several farms that were abandoned to avoid pollution of Langsett Reservoir. It is said that in 1588 the rent was a red rose at Christmas and a snowball in midsummer, but there is no mention of how, or if, the farmer ever managed to deliver these.

Kiddiwalks in the Peak District

3

trees and through a little wicket gate to a delightful spot by a clapper bridge over a stream.

3 Return to the little gate and turn right to walk high above the Little Don River. Then, descending to river level, you stroll through a plantation. Another little gate leads to a flight of steps; then you fork right up a narrow path.

4 Rejoining the *pushchair walk*, the track descends past a grassy area, sheltered by sycamores, the site of Brookhouse Farm, which was abandoned in 1907. The forest track on the left is the return route, but first continue down the cobbles to the stone Brookhouse Bridge and a great picnic and paddling spot. This is the ancient Cut Gate track, which linked the Derwent Valley farms with Penistone market. Returning to the broad path, this leads back through trees planted in the 1920s to stabilise the steep Langsett Bank. As you near the car park, stay on the lower path, which leads into Langsett village, and join the road near the valve house. Do you think it looks like a castle? Turn left, and go left again past Bank View café and the Waggon and Horses. Then, keeping left, you walk through some very nice houses, back to Langsett Barn.

◆ Fun Things to See and Do ◆

The walk goes to an old stone bridge by a lovely picnic and **paddling spot** (Brookhouse Bridge). The **trees at Langsett** are mainly pine and larch. The children will enjoy gathering the cones and if you take a tree book they can help identify the species from the shape of the cones. Larch cones are smaller and more rounded. Pines keep their needles all year, but larch is deciduous and in spring you can find its little red brush-like flowers.

There are several **drystone walls** in the forest, which are cleverly made without mortar. Look for **gritstone gateposts** that remain standing in the forest, showing where there were once fields. You may spot some **nesting boxes**, put there to encourage the woodland birds.

Crook Hill

A Climb to Twin Rocky Peaks

On Crook Hill.

Some people aspire to climb Everest, while others aim for Mont Blanc, Snowdon or Scafell Pike, but the essence of a good expedition is that it should have an objective. Now while the Peak District is often referred to as The Peak, there are very few true summits and those with rocky spires clawing towards the sky are almost as rare as hens' teeth. But Crook Hill is one of those few and a fine summit it is, with twin gritstone tops requiring enough scrambling to reward any child. Up here the view is superb, with the magnificent wilderness of Bleaklow stretching to the far horizon, while below gleam the blue waters of Ladybower.

Kiddiwalks in the Peak District

4

Getting there *The Derwent Valley is signed from the A57. Follow the road beside Ladybower Reservoir.*

Length of walk 4 miles.
Time Allow 4 hours.
Terrain Some rough paths, with a scramble to the summit. **NB:** Though the Crook Hill rocks are fun to explore there are some dizzy drops.
Start/Parking Hurst Clough free car park (GR 187876).
Map OS Explorer OL1 – Dark Peak area.
Refreshments There is a visitor centre and café at Fairholmes,

about 2 miles further up the valley.

1 From Hurst Clough car park go down the grassy bank and turn left. The stepped path crosses Hurst Clough between the two huge pipes of the aqueduct carrying water from Derwent Reservoir to the treatment works. The black metal domes, looking a bit like Daleks, are air outlets for these pipes. How many Daleks do we see on this walk? The path continues through the trees, where bluebells bloom in spring. Emerging into the open, continue along the path. Can you pick out

The Walk

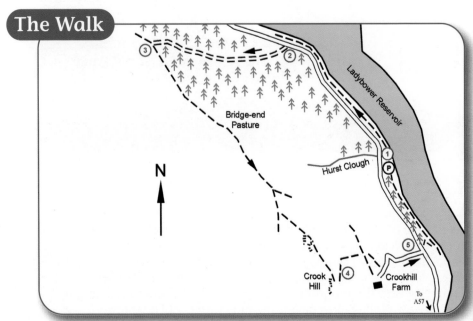

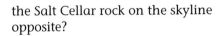

the Salt Cellar rock on the skyline opposite?

2 Reaching a wooden gate, opposite the submerged site of Derwent village, cross the road to Bridge End car park and follow the rough track up through the trees. This was the old pack road.

Once hazelnuts were harvested at Derwent and brought this way to Glossop. The conifers though are recent, planted to reduce the amount of soil washed into the reservoirs.

3 At the top of the hill you emerge into the open and turn

◆ Fun Things to See and Do ◆

The highlight of the walk is the **scramble up Crook Hill** and a photo of the children on the summit is a must. You may see **waterfowl on the reservoir** and will certainly hear lots of birdsong in the woods, so be sure and take the binoculars. Look for and try to identify the **many different trees** in the woodland. They are not all larch, pine and spruce as some broadleaved native trees have also been planted. The children will enjoy collecting fir cones.

Afterwards you can continue to **Fairholmes car park** (fee paying), which has a visitor centre, and a café serving ice creams, drinks and snacks. The chaffinches are very tame (we've had them perch on our hands) and there are lots of ducks to feed and a biodiversity pole. How many different species can you see on the pole? You can also hire cycles (telephone: 01433 651261).

You may like to walk a little further along the road to visit **Tip's Memorial**. In December 1953 a Derwent shepherd, Joseph Tagg, was lost on the Howden Moors. It was thirteen weeks before his body was discovered and beside it was his dog Tip, still standing guard. Although nursed back to health, Tip sadly died a year later and subscriptions for a memorial came from all over the world.

left. The grassy bridleway leads beside the trees and then continues over Bridge-end Pasture, which was once a high sheep walk, 'Pasturam de Cruchill', an important possession of the medieval Welbeck Abbey. The twin peaks of Crook Hill are ahead and on the skyline to the left is the outcrop of Wheel Stones or 'Coach and Horses' – can you see why? Descending to a signpost you fork right beside the wall on the bridleway to Snake Road. A wooden gate leads onto the access land and, turning left, you make a summit bid for Crook Hill. After scrambling up through the rocks to the flat top at 1,253 ft, an easy

path leads across the intervening col (dip) to the slightly lower summit, whose rocky top is very spectacular, with views across Ladybower Reservoir to Win Hill's heathery slopes, while westwards lies Kinder.

4 Now return to the col and, turning right, descend to the right of way. A gate by a signpost leads into a field and you take the waymarked National Trust concession path, which avoids the Crookhill farmyard, slanting down to join the metalled farm track.

5 Continue down to the road, then go left. Just past the bus turning circle an old track leads down to a seat with a poem. To the right is the magnificent Ashopton Viaduct; this appears as a low bridge, but old photographs show its newly built pillars towering 70 ft above the site of the former village of Ashopton. The villagers were rehoused in a new community at Yorkshire Bridge, lower down the valley. Now turn left beside the reservoir for a gentle stroll through tall larches back to Hurst Clough.

Background Notes ◆

Crook comes from the Old English 'croc', meaning land in a bend. Yet though the River Ashop has been swallowed by thirsty Sheffield, Derby, Leicester and Nottingham, whose citizens do a good job of disposing of the rain which amounts to over four feet a year, the bend in Ladybower Reservoir remains.

Howden and Derwent came first, in 1901; then **Ladybower**, which destroyed Derwent village and the hamlet of Ashopton, was begun in 1935, but not completed for another ten years. In dry weather the ruins of the houses appear again as the reservoir drops to only a small fraction of its full complement of 6,300 million gallons.

The **dams of Derwent and Howden reservoirs** were used for training the 617 Dambusters squadron during the Second World War and an occasional RAF plane still flies down the valley.

Lantern Pike

Extensive Views from a Heathery Hill

On the descent from Lantern Pike.

It hasn't got a lantern and it doesn't look much like a pike, but you can see why Lantern Pike was the site of an Armada beacon, for the view in every direction stretches for miles. There's a topograph indicating what you can see and on it is inscribed a memorial to Edwin Royce, who died in 1946 – 'In memory of his labour in the cause of securing freedom of the hills'. It was 58 years before the cause he held so dear was finally achieved with the Countryside and Rights of Way Act, which came into force on 19th September 2004. And what a place to put his memorial, for the skyline is filled with the high open moors where now all have the right to walk.

Lantern Pike

Getting there *Hayfield is 4 miles south of Glossop on the A624.*

Length of walk 3½ miles.
Time About 4 hours.
Terrain The Sett Valley Trail (see map) is very good for pushchairs, but the rest of the walk involves a steep climb and some of the paths are quite rough and narrow.
Start/Parking Sett Valley Trail pay and display car park on the site of Hayfield Station, a few yards along the A6015. (GR 036869). Toilets and visitor centre.
Map OS Explorer OL1 – Dark Peak area.
Refreshments Hayfield has several pubs and cafés.

1 Set off along the Sett Valley Trail, which leads through the trees and past a bluebell wood. Off to the right you can see the heathery point of Lantern Pike and soon you look down on Birch Vale Reservoir.

2 After nearly a mile of easy walking turn right, down beside a factory, and cross the reservoir dam. Can you see any ducks? The path crosses the River Sett and climbs the hillside. Then, meeting a track, you turn left. Follow the track round the bend and, joining the Pennine Bridleway, climb up to Sitch Lane and Windy Knowle Cottages.

Fun Things to See and Do

With the help of **the hill indicator on the summit of Lantern Pike** you can identify all the surrounding landmarks from Black Hill in the north, over Kinder and Bleaklow in the east, to Axe Edge far to the south.

Hayfield Visitor Centre has a selection of leaflets and guides and you pass several interesting information boards on the walk. The **Calico Trail** board at point 6 tells the story of Swallow House Well, the only water supply for Lucas Terrace opposite, built in 1853 to house the workers of Wood Mill. Just imagine having to cross the road and carry all the water needed for cooking, cleaning and washing back home after a 12-hour shift at the mill.

The Walk

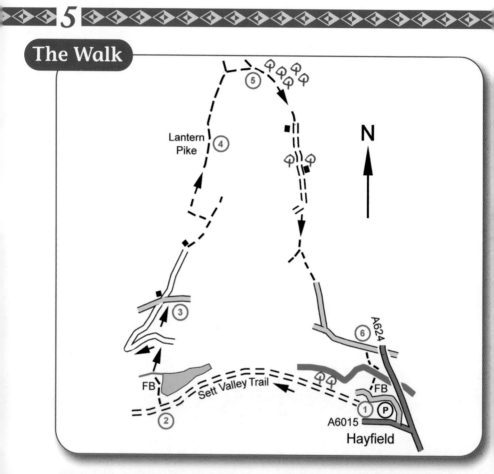

❸ Go straight across the junction and follow the bridleway up the hill. Continue climbing past Sunny Side and on reaching the NT Lantern Pike notice you turn left. Follow the path up beside the wall through the heather, then along the top of the ridge.

❹ Despite its lowly status Lantern Pike has extensive views in all directions. You then continue along the path, which descends to rejoin the Pennine Bridleway. A surfaced strip leads across the field; then a path keeps straight on, slanting down to the field corner.

❺ Descending past Hey Wood, you continue down beneath a bank of bilberry bushes. On reaching Firbob Cottage, follow the track across the hillside,

with a bird's-eye view of Little Hayfield, and continue past the aptly named Cliffbank Farm. Keeping straight on at the bend the path goes above a steep, wooded slope, where you can look for acorns in autumn. When you reach a wooden kissing gate, fork left and continue descending into Bank Vale, whose 19th-century paper mill is long gone. Continue along the tarmac lane and on reaching Swallow House Lane turn left.

6 Just before the bypass bridge look for the well belonging to Swallow House by the Calico Trail information board. The walk continues through the park, then crosses a wooden footbridge over the River Sett. Finally you follow the path back, through the houses, to the old Hayfield station.

Background Notes ◆

The Hayfield railway line was built for the Midland & Great Central Joint Railway Company and opened in 1868. The line lasted just over a century, eventually closing in 1970, and is now the **Sett Valley Trail**. From the old station, now Hayfield Information Centre, the Trail gives easy walking beneath a canopy of trees to New Mills and The Torrs.

The **River Sett** feeds Birch Vale Reservoir, which was built in the 1750s to provide water power for Birch Vale Calico Printworks. Several woollen and cotton mills were powered by the river, corn was ground in a common mill and, by the mid-19th century, there were three print works and two paper mills. The walk passes mill workers' cottages at **Bank Vale**, a very attractive spot. **Clough Mill**, in the hamlet of Little Hayfield, is an early 19th-century cotton mill, now converted into flats. In the 1830s this was the scene of riots when hordes of armed workers marched here from Glossop to demand higher wages.

Hayfield village, now bypassed by the busy A624, was in the medieval parish of Glossop and a chapel was built here in 1386. An important packhorse route led eastwards over the moors by Edale Cross to Edale.

Mam Tor

The Shivering Mountain

Everyone knows that, worn away by ice, snow and wind, eventually mountains fall down. But Mam Tor is doing it in real time. They call it the 'Shivering Mountain', for this wonder of the Peak is made of a crumbling sandwich of gritstone and shale, whose steep face is in constant movement. Even modern engineering is powerless, and forty years ago the A625 was abandoned after a final cataclysmic upheaval. Children will love the road that looks like the results of an earthquake, where they can stand astride chasms and see in profile the layer upon layer of tarmac laid by engineers as they struggled to save the highway. But the walk starts off uphill with a climb to a summit surrounded by the ramparts of a hill fort. Well, not quite surrounded as part of it now lies at the bottom, for even in the Iron Age the hill was falling down!

Mam Tor

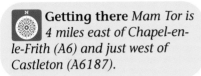

Getting there *Mam Tor is 4 miles east of Chapel-en-le-Frith (A6) and just west of Castleton (A6187).*

Length of walk 2½ miles.
Time About 3 hours.
Terrain A very steep ascent up steps. The descent may be boggy.

Start/Parking Above Castleton, near the top of Winnats Pass. Follow signs to Blue John Cavern. Roadside parking (GR 128832).
Map OS Explorer OL1 – Dark Peak area.
Refreshments Take a picnic or visit one of the many cafés and pubs in Castleton.

Fun Things to See and Do ◆

You will probably see **hang-gliders and paragliders** soaring in the up-currents high above Mam Tor. The children will enjoy watching them taking off and landing.

When you reach **Hollins Cross** look down on the mill far below in the Edale valley and imagine what it would be like for the people of Castleton who had to climb over this ridge to get to work every day.

See if you can pick out the 12th-century **Pevril Castle**, high above Castleton, which is well worth a visit later.

The last bit of the walk gives a good view of the alternate layers of **grit and shale** that make up the precipitous face of Mam Tor.

Afterwards you can visit **Blue John Cavern**, whose decorative stone has been prized since the 18th century. The name probably derives from the French bleu-jaune, meaning blue yellow. It is a form of coloured fluorspar, from which small ornaments and jewellery are made, though in the past large pieces were used to produce vases and even a candelabra. There are three more show caves in Castleton, **Peak Cavern, Treak Cliff Cavern and Speedwell Cavern**, and also the splendid new £1 million **Castleton Centre**, which houses the museum and information centre.

The Walk

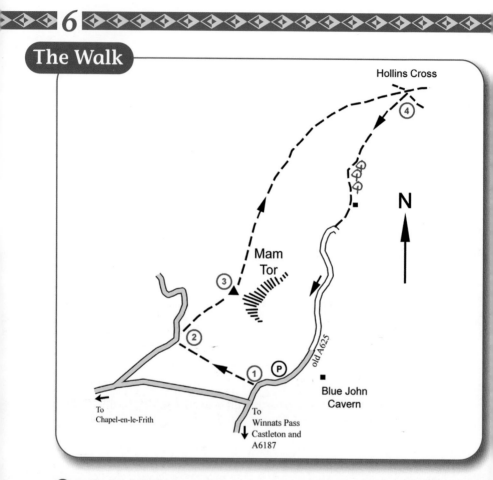

1 Take the footpath signed 'Mam Tor summit', which sets off uphill about 100 yards from the road junction. This leads through an area of 18th-century lead mine workings and it's a steep grassy ascent to the road at Mam Nick.

2 A long flight of shallow steps now climbs Mam Tor, with the excuse of looking at the view back over Rushup Edge as you

pause for breath. Look out for the earth ditches and ramparts of the Iron Age hill fort as you near the top. To the right the fortifications have fallen over the edge.

3 The summit is crowned by a trig point and paved to protect it from the hundreds of visitors who make the ascent every year. The Great Ridge now stretches on ahead to Back Tor and Lose Hill

beyond, while northwards lies the vast expanse of Kinder. You can also pick out the tall chimney of the Hope Cement Works in the pastoral fields of Hope Valley. The next mile is easy – just follow the flagged path downhill.

4 On reaching the stone bollard at Hollins Cross, turn right and take the rightmost fork. The rough little path slants down across the hillside through the gorse, then keeps above the trees. A narrow path winds round the hillside to join the old road; then you walk up past landslips where the road has crumpled and fallen away beneath the dramatic cliff face of Mam Tor. Finally you pass the entrance to Blue John Cavern to return to the start.

Background Notes ◆

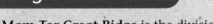

Mam Tor Great Ridge is the division between the gentler limestone hills of the central Peak District and the wild moorland of the north.

Encircling the summit of Mam Tor are the defensive ramparts of an **Iron Age hill fort**, though much of the eastern side has vanished over the edge. This was the home of Celtic people 2000 years ago.

At **Mam Nick** the narrow road from the south crosses between Rushup Edge and Mam Tor, before winding its way down to Edale. The hummocky slopes of Rushup Edge were caused at the end of the Ice Age when the surface layers slipped downhill over the still frozen ground.

Hollins Cross, the lowest point on the Great Ridge, is marked by a circular stone memorial, erected in 1964. Here an old packhorse way crossed the ridge. It was used in the 18th century by Castleton mill girls making their daily journey on foot, in all weathers, to work in Edale Spinning Mill, which can still be seen far below.

The **A625**, the old main road into Castleton, lost the battle and being beyond repair was eventually closed in 1979 before sliding downhill in its final collapse.

7

Higger Tor and Carl Wark

Rocky Tors and a Hill Fort

Building a fort in the Iron Age started with choosing the right place and the isolated rocky knoll of Carl Wark, high above Hathersage, was ideal. Steep rocky slopes on three sides made it very difficult for an enemy to approach. But there was one weakness, for on the northern side you could just stroll up and walk straight in. So they built a wall. But this was no ordinary wall. Over the years many large castles have disappeared completely as the local population took the stones away to build their houses, but the stones of Carl Wark are absolutely enormous. 'Up with your end Fred' certainly wasn't a feasible approach, it must have taken dozens of men to inch these huge boulders into position. And here they still are. So when the children are out of puff from the descent of Higger Tor, see who fancies climbing straight up Carl Wark when at the top there's a lot of angry men waving spears.

Higger Tor and Carl Wark

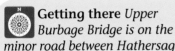

Getting there *Upper Burbage Bridge is on the minor road between Hathersage and Sheffield.*

Length of walk 3 miles.
Time About 3 hours.
Terrain Some good paths, but the descent from Higger Tor is a rocky scramble. Only Duke's Drive is suitable for pushchairs (see map).

NB: The rocky tors have some steep drops.
Start/Parking The free car park at Upper Burbage Bridge (GR 260830).
Map OS Explorer OL1 – Dark Peak area.
Refreshments If you are lucky there will be an ice cream van in the car park, but there are cafés and pubs in Hathersage.

Fun Things to See and Do ♦

The sheep begging for food at Burbage Packhorse Bridge are very tame; they may even let you stroke them.

There are **lots of boulders** to scramble on and jump off and the children can practise walking up huge, flat, rocky slabs.

Burbage Brook is excellent for paddling, with the additional challenge of wading under the bridge.

If you venture into the plantation **compare the vegetation**. It is completely different, with the ground covered in fir cones and pine needles instead of bracken and heather.

Look out for the numerous small holes in the boulders of **Burbage Rocks**. These are bullet scars from Second World War army training exercises. There will probably be lots of climbers here. How many can you see?

Finish off the day in **Hathersage** with a visit to Little John's grave in the churchyard. There are several outdoor pursuit shops stocking the latest children's walking gear and, a rarity nowadays, there's an outdoor swimming pool.

The Walk

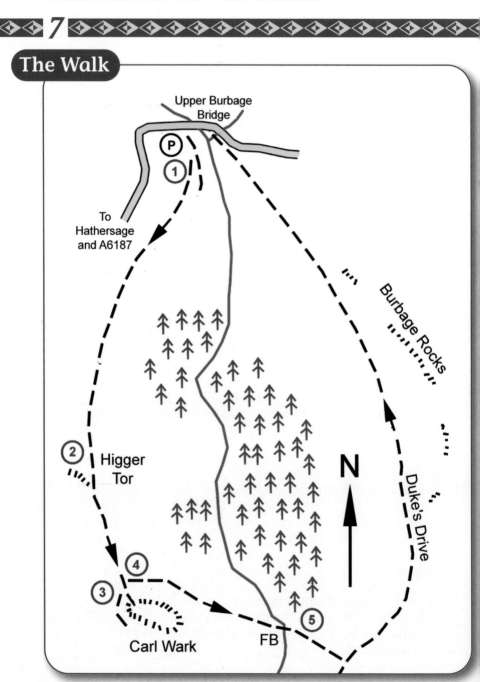

Upper Burbage Bridge

P

1

To Hathersage and A6187

Burbage Rocks

2
Higger Tor

N

Duke's Drive

4

3

5

Carl Wark

FB

Higger Tor and Carl Wark

1 Take the footpath onto the access land from the Hathersage side of Upper Burbage Bridge, then fork right. The broad path leads through the heather high above the valley and then curves away above a plantation, dipping down before heading up steps to the rocky outcrop of Higger Tor.

2 The flat top is strewn with rocks and weirdly eroded boulders

– but *take care* above the precipitous cliffs. It is a good viewpoint and to the west lies the Vale of Edale where you can see the 439 ft chimney of Hope Cement Works. At the far end of the tor you pick your way down through the jumbled boulders and then follow the obvious path to Carl Wark.

3 Climbing to meet the defensive wall that edges this side

Background Notes ◆

Carl Wark was obviously a fort, though whether it was Iron Age or refortified at the end of the Roman period is less clear, but it must have been a good defensive position and is a superb vantage point, looking down on Burbage Brook and the valley below. It is thought to be between 2,500 and 3,500 years old.

Through a geologist's eye, these **isolated gritstone knolls** to the south of Stanage Edge and facing Burbage Edge across the valley of Burbage Brook are outcrops of hard gritstone, left behind as the encircling softer rock weathered away. Although the process continues today, it must have been more rapid towards the end of the Ice Age, with successive freeze and thaw and the harsh effect of sand blown by the wind from bare rocky surfaces.

Burbage packhorse bridge is thought to be on the line of an old Roman road from the fort at Brough to another in Sheffield.

Duke's Drive was a private road built in the 19th century to access his grouse moors by the Duke of Rutland, who had a shooting lodge on the Longshaw Estate.

of Carl Wark, you turn right beside these huge blocks to reach an information plaque. A few steps further on there is an old gritstone stone trough carved in situ. Now climb up onto the top and look for the original entrance to the fort, where the gritstone wall turns inwards. From here you can pick out Owler Tor, to the south-west, and the tall mast on Sir William Hill.

4 Now retrace your steps on the Higger Tor path to the bottom of the slope and turn right. Several grassy paths lead down into the valley and they all meet up at the little 18th-century

packhorse bridge at the forest corner. Why doesn't the bridge have parapets? It is to leave room for the packhorse panniers.

5 Cross Burbage Brook, then keep straight on up the steps, beside the plantation, and fork right. On reaching Duke's Drive, turn left; then it's an obvious track all the way back, passing below the steep rocky buttresses of Burbage Rocks. When you get to the road there is an interesting information board, and staying below Upper Burbage Bridge the children can step across a couple of streams, back to the car park.

Baslow Edge

Woodland and Water

Walking along Baslow Edge.

The children really ought to wear wellingtons on this walk. Not because it's wet and muddy, it isn't, in fact the stroll through the heather and back along the edge is one of the easiest walks in the book, but here is a monument to the inventor of the famous boot. It wasn't of course the only thing the great general did; there's the small matter of Waterloo in 1815. The gritstone pinnacle was erected by Baslow's local doctor, a retired Indian Army man himself, to complement the one to Admiral Nelson across the valley. Then on the way back you explore the edge. Keep a tight hold on the more venturesome, for edge it certainly is, but peering cautiously over you get a real feel of what rock climbing is all about.

Kiddiwalks in the Peak District

Getting there *Curbar Gap is 2 miles north of Baslow. Turn off the A623 at Calver and follow Curbar Lane to the top of the hill, or turn off the A621 and head north-west.*

Length of walk 1½ miles.
Time Up to 2 hours.
Terrain The walk starts on a broad path, suitable for pushchairs as far as the Eagle Stone, but the return is along a narrow, rocky footpath. **NB:** Steep unfenced drops along Baslow Edge.
Start/Parking Curbar Gap pay and display car park (GR 262747).
Map OS Explorer OL 24 – White Peak area.

Refreshments Take a picnic. There may be an ice cream van in the car park if you are lucky.

1 Take the wheelchair path, which leads from the Curbar side of Curbar Gap car park. Cross the road and follow the track towards Baslow Edge. Can the children work out how to open the wooden gate, and what does the sign on the tree say? Now set off along the track over Eaglestone Flat that follows the wall, then keep straight on through the heather. Why do you think this was once an old road?

2 It is quite safe here for children to run on ahead to the huge Eagle Stone, which proves impossibly difficult to climb.

◆ Fun Things to See and Do ◆

There are **lots of rocks** to scramble up and jump off, big flat rocks to walk across, rocks that resemble strange creatures, and overhanging rocks that make secret caves.

The children can look for the natural, **eroded rock hollows** that are usually full of water and find **half-finished millstones** on Baslow Edge.

There is an **information board** in the Curbar Gap car park, but don't miss the **guide stone** which is over the wall near the car park entrance.

The Walk

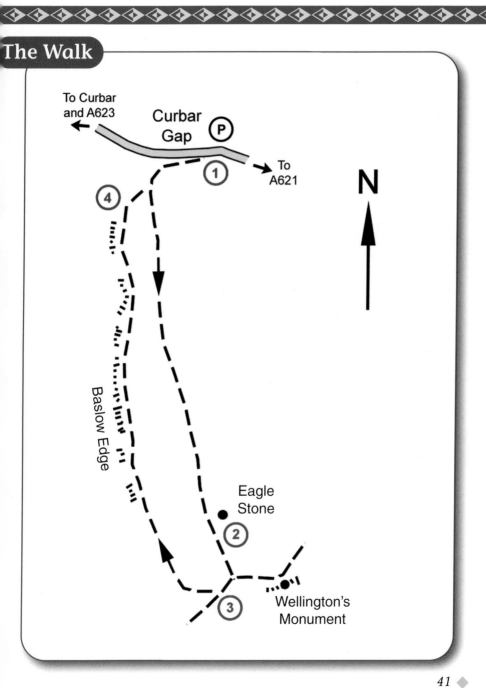

At the Eagle Stone.

Continue along the track to the edge of the moor and turn left along the old packhorse way to Wellington's Monument, a good picnic spot with a convenient seat. There is an inscription to decipher, and you may be able to spot the tiny finger of Nelson's Monument on the far side of the valley, above Gardom's Edge.

3 Now walk back along the edge and, ignoring the Eagle Stone track, take the little path on the right that wanders along the edge above the unfenced steep drops of Bar Quarry. This is where the stone for many of the houses in Baslow was obtained. The narrow path, with magnificent views, leads through bracken, heather and bilberry along the shapely escarpment of Baslow Edge, high above the village of Baslow. You wander through weirdly-shaped wind-eroded rocks, while below the edge are one or two partly finished millstones, abandoned when the market collapsed in the 19th century.

4 On arriving at the wheelchair viewpoint, you will find a neatly labelled panorama, so it is easy to identify landmarks. Then follow the surfaced path, back to Curbar Gap.

◆ Background Notes ◆

Old packhorse ways crossed at Curbar Gap, a natural dip in the gritstone ridge between Curbar Edge and Baslow Edge. One of these was the packhorse route to Chesterfield, which carried salt, and it zigzagged its way up to the edge, where there's a jagger's (pack-horseman's) guidepost. This is carefully marked on all four faces, and also signed and dated 1709. Understandably the supervisor wanted there to be no doubt that he had complied with the 1702 Act of Parliament requiring all such junctions to be marked.

The **Eagle Stone** is the largest glacial deposit of gritstone in the Peak and was once a meeting place for packhorse trains where jaggers haggled over goods, so it is also known as the Haggle Stone. There is a doubtful story which says that the bachelors of Baslow were required to climb to the top of it before they could marry. They must have been very agile, for the huge gritstone block is no easy scramble, even for a rock climber.

The inscription on **Wellington's Monument**, 'Erected 1866 by E.M. Wrench late 34th Reg'mt', implies a military tribute and indeed Dr Wrench served in the Indian Army. Although the monument faces the tiny finger of Nelson's Monument, it was put up nearly sixty years later, and some fourteen years after the Iron Duke's death in 1852. Chiefly remembered for the Battle of Waterloo, the general said: 'Nothing except a battle lost can be half so melancholy as a battle won.'

The **northernmost tip of Baslow Edge** is a fine viewpoint and close by is one of the strangest notice boards in the Peak District. 'No manure removal', it commands, so we told the little one to wipe her red wellington boots.

9

Cressbrook Dale

Flowers and a Scramble

Having fun on the stepping stones.

hy does anyone need to count up to a hundred? Well, one of the reasons is Cressbrook Dale. This is a flower hunter's delight, where, in spring, early purple orchids mass across its slopes, while later in the year you'll find rock roses, bloody cranesbill and thyme. If the children count all the different flowers they'll certainly need to be able to go a lot higher than ten. There's a fenced mineshaft and a tunnel on the hillside, and then comes Peter's Stone. This is a mountain in miniature. Defended on all sides by vertical rock, its summit is not easily attained, but with care you can scramble up by its one weakness. Here on the very top you look down on the valley below from the place where they held the last public execution in the Peak District. Well at least the man had a good view.

Cressbrook Dale

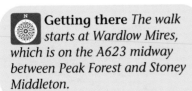

Getting there *The walk starts at Wardlow Mires, which is on the A623 midway between Peak Forest and Stoney Middleton.*

Length of walk 2 miles.
Time About 2 hours.
Terrain Some rough and some easy paths.

Start/Parking The A623 layby at Wardlow Mires, west of the junction with the B6465 (GR 179756).
Map OS Explorer OL 24 – White Peak area.
Refreshments Take a picnic. After your walk you could visit Litton (turn south off the A623 to the west of Wardlow Mires), where you will find the Red Lion on the

Fun Things to See and Do ◆

There are several **old trial levels** (experimental tunnels) that can be explored, as they only extend for a few yards.

There are a couple of **stepstiles** to climb, and the more adventurous, under careful supervision, can venture to the top of **Peter's Stone**.

The **stepping stones** were a great success on our visit despite the fact that there was, as usual, no water! Where has the water gone? In winter it's here, but in summer the river flows underground.

The glory of the dale is the **flowers**, and older children will enjoy finding the names from a flower book. This is also a walk for those interested in **birds**, and May is the best month for birdsong.

If there is time, complete the day with a visit to **Tideswell** (on the B6049 to the west of Wardlow Mires). The long main street zigzags past the magnificent 14th-century Tideswell church, known as the Cathedral of the Peak, the finest in the whole area, and from it a maze of little lanes spreads up towards old lead workings on the hillside above. There is also a very good children's playground.

The Walk

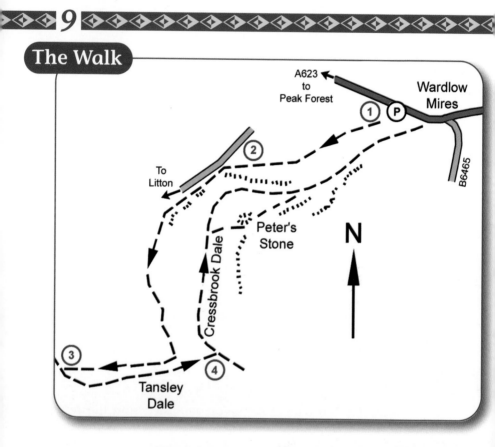

village green and the Post Office Café, or go on to Tideswell, which has several pubs and cafés.

1 From the layby go through the little wooden gate at the head of Cressbrook Dale and, forking right, climb up beside the wall across flower-filled grassy slopes. On reaching a stile, walk across the field to the opposite corner and then go back onto the edge of the dale and continue beside the wall.

2 At the road, turn left and continue beside the wall, high above the dale. There are lovely views down into the dale and across to Peter's Stone, but *take care*, for the ground drops away steeply. When you reach the next stile, ask the children what they think the wooden post is for. It's a dog gate, which little ones can crawl through. The path now goes sharp right and continues beside the wall, past a dewpond cleverly constructed

to serve two fields. A fenced enclosure hides the awesome chasm of a mineshaft – why is there a ruin here?

3 On reaching the corner, go left and stroll down narrow Tansley Dale. The path leads down the flower-filled dale between limestone cliffs and past old mine workings, whose spoil is smothered in early summer with the tiny white flowers of leadwort.

4 At the little gate at the bottom, cross the stepping stones and turn left up Cressbrook Dale, past several trial mine entrances. The slightly higher path is more interesting for children and you can have a race. Peter's Stone soon dominates the valley and older children will enjoy a supervised climb to the top. Below the rocky tor is the best spot for early purple orchids. On reaching the end of the dale, cut back across the grass, to the layby.

Background Notes ◆

Cressbrook Dale has a variety of wildlife habitats ranging from limestone grassland to ash woodland and clear streams. May and June are the best months for flowers, when you will find early purple orchids in abundance.

Tansley Dale has leadmine spoil covered in the starry flowers of leadwort, otherwise known as spring sandwort. This is one of the few flowers that can tolerate lead contamination of the soil.

At first sight **Peter's Stone**, an isolated turret of rock that dominates the head of Cressbrook Dale, appears impregnable, with its vertical limestone sides, but a steep gully cleaves the rock, providing an easy scramble to the top. Although Methodist meetings were once held here, the place is chiefly famous as the site of a hanging when, in 1815, a local murderer was executed and his body left suspended from a gibbet on the rock. After murdering a woman who was a toll gate keeper he gave her shoes to another woman he fancied, which led immediately to his detection.

10

Goyt Valley

A Walk Back in Time

Ruins are often better than stately houses as far as children are concerned. There are no ropes marked 'Do not cross', and no fretful supervisors telling them to be quiet. But if they are quiet they might just hear the echoes of the past, as Errwood Hall rang to the sound of happy laughter when Samuel Grimshawe and his family lived here. In the surrounding woods they planted thousands of rhododendrons, brought back on the family's ocean going yacht, and in spring, as you walk up the long drive through woods, bright with their purple flowers and the air filled with the heavy scent of yellow azaleas, it is easy for a moment to imagine yourself back in the 19th century. So stand for a minute on the lawn and visualise Miss Dolores, the Spanish governess, watching from the three arched windows that remain of this once lovely hall.

◇◇◇◇◇◇◇◇◇◇◇◇◇◇◇◇◇◇◇◇◇◇◇

Getting there *The Goyt Valley lies between Whaley Bridge and Buxton, and is signed from the A5004. (NB: Errwood Hall cannot be reached from the south via Derbyshire Bridge because of a one-way system – see below.)*

Length of walk 1 mile.
Time Allow 1½ hours.
Terrain Easy paths, but pushchairs are feasible only as far as Errwood Hall (see map).
Start/Parking Errwood Hall free car park (GR 012748). Traffic is one way only from Errwood up to Derbyshire Bridge throughout the year. On Sundays and bank holidays from 1st May to the end of September the road from Errwood dam to Derbyshire Bridge is closed to traffic, so park at The Street car park (GR 014756) by Errwood Dam and walk down the road towards Errwood Hall (this adds an extra mile to the walk).
Map OS Explorer OL 24 – White Peak area.
Refreshments Take a picnic.

1 From the notice board at the back of Errwood Hall car park a sign points to the 'Errwood Hall Woodland Walk'. Follow the path uphill, forking right through a gap in the wall. A broad track leads gently down through the trees and then

The Walk

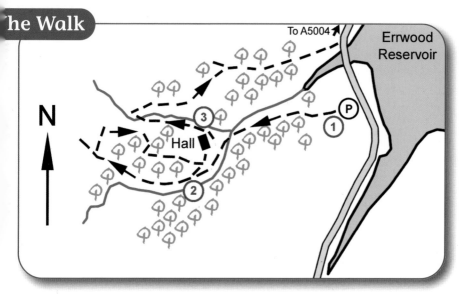

To A5004
Errwood Reservoir
N
Hall
P
3
1
2

climbs above the stream, with an unfenced drop on one side. Errwood Hall is just off to the right at the junction ahead.

2 If you don't mind a bit more climbing keep straight on, past a couple of tall gateposts and a shaley bank, the site of an old coal pit, to the ruined Castedge cottages. Turn right, signed 'cemetery', and climb on past the yew trees to the hilltop and burial ground. After reading the inscriptions and admiring the view, cross the flat-topped hill and follow the grassy path, which descends steeply through the rhododendrons. Then turn left on the stepped track to Errwood Hall.

3 Walk on past the ruins; then steps take you down to a long boardwalk by the stream, a good paddling spot. Follow the path, which curves right up the steps,

◆ Fun Things to See and Do ◆

Explore the ruins of Errwood Hall and try to imagine what it would have been like when the Grimshawes lived here. The layout of downstairs remains, so children could decide what each room was used for. Why do you think the hall was demolished? It was to make sure that water flowing into the reservoir was not contaminated.

In the **burial ground** you will find the grave of John Butler, Captain of the yacht *Mariquita*, 'For 16 years the friend and faithful servant of the late Samuel Grimshawe'. There is also the grave of a young French maid. You can admire the view and look over to Wild Moor and see where the heather has been burnt in strips to regenerate new shoots for both sheep and grouse to feed on.

In the **woodland** the native oak, birch and rowan are mixed with Sitka spruce, larch and lodgepole pine. Over **70 different species of bird** have been identified in the Goyt Valley, including woodpeckers, jays, finches, tree pipits. You may even spot the rarer crossbill. Birds of prey include tawny owl, sparrowhawk and goshawk, while, if you are lucky, you could see red deer, stoats, foxes or brown hares.

(don't cross the footbridge) and continue beside the fence, signed 'Woodland Walk'. The path leads across the hillside to a T-junction where you turn downhill, above the rhododendrons. Here you can look out for the huge leaves of the sweet chestnut. The broad path leads down to the road, where you turn right, over an arm of Errwood Reservoir, back to the car park.

On the path by the reservoir.

Background Notes ◆

The Victorian mansion of **Errwood Hall** was a family home built by the industrialist Samuel Grimshawe as a wedding present for his son in 1830. There was a village community, centred around the 300 year old Goyt Bridge, with cottages, a private school for about thirty children, a watermill, and even a small coal mine.

Stones beside the track are the ruins of estate workers' cottages, while grass-covered mounds hint at the once formal gardens, but the **acres of rhododendrons and azaleas** that the Grimshawes brought back from their travels are still a powerful reminder of the days of splendour. Over 40,000 rhododendrons were used as ballast in their ocean going yacht and then planted in the grounds along with pine, oak and beech trees.

In the Grimshawes' hilltop **burial ground** the members of the family and some of their servants are buried, including the captain of their yacht. The hall was demolished in 1938 when Fernilee Reservoir was constructed, and Mrs Gosselin, the last of the family, died in 1930.

Errwood Reservoir was completed in 1967 to supplement Stockport's water supply, and a new road was built. You can see the flooded drive to Errwood Hall beneath the concrete bridge.

Lud's Church

A Hiding Place in the Woods

A ncient mansions may have their priest holes and secret rooms, but in the woods near Gradbach is one of the most magnificent natural hiding places in the Peak District. It doesn't look like a church. It isn't even man made, but this is where the persecuted Lollards and their leader Walter de Ludauk came to worship in the 14th century. At first acquaintance you might think it was a collapsed cave, but this deep ravine was formed when the entire hillside slipped towards the River Dane, leaving an enormous gash. Steps lead down into the depths where you look up the sheer, mossy walls to the strip of sky above and marvel how Squire Trafford of Swythamley, coming at full gallop and unable to stop, spurred his horse to leap. But perhaps children would prefer to be Sir Gawain, for this is the legendary Green Chapel in an early medieval poem, where he came to challenge the Green Knight.

Lud's Church

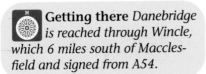 **Getting there** *Danebridge is reached through Wincle, which 6 miles south of Maccles-field and signed from A54.*

Length of walk 4½ miles.
Time Allow a good 4 hours.
Terrain Rough paths that can be muddy but boardwalks avoid the worst bits.
Start/Parking Roadside parking beyond the Ship Inn at Danebridge (GR 964652).
Map OS Explorer OL 24 – White Peak area.
Refreshments The Ship Inn, near the start of the walk, has a beer garden.

1 Cross the high, arched bridge over the River Dane and turn left, signed 'Gradbach'. The track leads down through the trees to the river, past a section of exposed rock layers, which are good for a geology lesson, then the waymarked path continues across the field. Climbing to a stile into a bluebell wood, the path heads round the hillside through the larches and pines. As you emerge into fields at a wooden stile the pointed cone of Shutlingsloe comes into view.

2 Passing the scout cottage at Back Dane, follow the track to the

Fun Things to See and Do ◆

Castle Rocks is a good place for a stop. Created by a landslip, the rocks are great for climbing. Even little ones can manage with a bit of help.

The highlight of the walk is the deep cleft of **Lud's Church**, which is great fun to explore.

Look for the two memorials on the **Hanging Stone**, especially our favourite, the one to Burke. Older children may be able to decipher them with assistance.

At the end of the walk the **River Dane meadow** can be revisited for a paddle and picnic, while **Back Forest** has prize-winning bilberries.

At **Danebridge Fisheries** children can feed the trout, and you can even catch your own supper with the use of farm tackle.

Kiddiwalks in the Peak District

The Walk

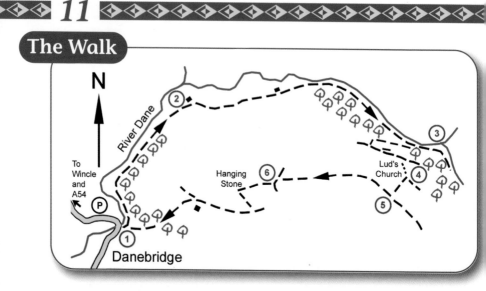

bend; then keep straight on. The waymarked path continues across the hillside and passes above an isolated house. What animals live here? The path now keeps straight on and goes down to the river; it then continues through the oak, silver birch and rowan trees of Back Forest. The unfenced path ambles along above the Dane, which flows in a deep gorge edged with high gritstone cliffs.

❸ When you reach a signpost in some tall Scots pine, turn sharp right and follow the path slanting back up the hillside. It's a steady climb, then the path bends left, to a signpost by the outcrop of Castle Rocks. Take the topmost path on the left, signed to Lud's Church, and let the children run

on ahead to find the rocky entrance.

❹ Steps lead down into the awesome chasm; then, at the far end, you take the right cleft, where more steps lead back up into the daylight. Follow the muddy path which continues across the hillside, through the trees, to a signpost, where you turn right up the concession path to the ridge. As the narrow path climbs through the heather the view opens out over the Dane Valley.

❺ At the top, turn right through the little wooden gate and follow the path, which switchbacks along the crest of the Back Forest ridge. From the rocky outcrop at the highest point you look across to Tittesworth Reservoir and the

scarp silhouette of Bosley Cloud, then it's a delightful downhill stroll.

6 On meeting a track, you turn left along the bridleway for a few yards; then go right over the stone stepstile and follow the concession path over the rough pasture to the Hanging Stone. Set on the very edge, this is a magnificent viewpoint. Gritstone steps lead down to the base of the massive buttress, where you pause to look at the inscriptions, then you follow the path down to join the track and turn right. Just beyond Hangingstone Farm turn left and follow the footpath down across the fields – a good spot for a race. Then, descending steeply through the wood, the path goes down the clough, back to the river and Danebridge.

Background Notes ◆

At one time **Lud's Church** was quite hard to find, its entrance concealed by a block of gritstone fallen across a narrow gap in the rocks; the trees grew thick about and there were no signposts. In those days wallabies roamed the area. They had escaped from a private zoo kept by Lt Col. Brocklehurst of Roaches Hall. His brother, who lived at Swythamley Hall, was Sir Philip Brocklehurst, who went to the South Pole with Shackleton. Sir Philip lost his toes through frostbite and kept them in a glass jar on his mantelpiece.

On the **Hanging Stone**, the most prominent of all the rock buttresses along the Back Forest ridge, Sir Philip erected a memorial to his brother. On the opposite face an older testimonial reads:

'Beneath this rock
August 1, 1874 was buried
BURKE
A Noble Mastiff
Black and Tan
Faithful as woman
Braver than man
A gun and a ramble
His heart's desire
With the friend of his life
The Swythamley Squire.'

The Hanging Stone.

Three Shires Head

A Paddle and a Picnic

Rivers are sometimes rather big and a bit scary, but here at Three Shires Head the River Dane is young. As it winds its way down from the high moors, then exuberantly tumbles under a packhorse bridge and over a waterfall, it is one of the most attractive places in the Peak District. But you start the walk by getting up close and personal with the Dane, for after descending through old gritstone quarries to the river's edge you have to step across. This is the fun bit, for children are usually less concerned about getting wet feet than Mums and Dads. Then when you arrive at Three Shires Head there's a bit of history, for this was once a hideaway for men from the nearby village of Flash who coined counterfeit money, knowing that escape was always to hand across the county boundary.

◇◆◇◆◇◆◇◆◇◆◇◆◇◆◇◆◇◆◇◆◇◆◇◆◇◆◇◆◇◆◇◆◇

Getting there *The starting point for this walk is 4 miles south-west of Buxton, on the A54.*

Length of walk 2½ miles.
Time Allow 2 hours plus paddling time.
Terrain An easy walk, rough in places, and gradually uphill all the way back. **NB:** The River Dane could be difficult to cross after heavy rain, and the fields below Holt Farm can be a bit boggy.
Start/Parking The roadside layby above the tall chimney (GR 008698).

Map OS Explorer OL 24 – White Peak area.
Refreshments Take a picnic. After the walk you can visit Blaze Farm, 3 miles south on the A54, which has a tearoom and a nature trail and offers home-made ice cream.

❶ About 50 yards beyond the Buxton end of the layby, take the grassy track which slants downhill. The path makes a steep and stony descent through the grass- and bilberry-covered mounds of Danebower Quarries, then kinks right at a signpost past

◆ Fun Things to See and Do ◆

With or without wellies **Three Shires Head** is a delightful spot for paddling. You can puzzle out which river bank is in Staffordshire and which in Cheshire and Derbyshire. It's not as easy as you might think. The children could also play at being smugglers, crossing from one county to another.

Have a look underneath the **old gritstone bridge** to see where it has been widened to take the increasing traffic, or perhaps to carry carts.

When you have finished the walk everyone would enjoy a visit to **Blaze Farm** for an ice cream and a play on the slide.

Buxton has a little train in the Pavilion Gardens, an indoor swimming pool, a selection of pubs and cafés and lots of shops.

The Walk

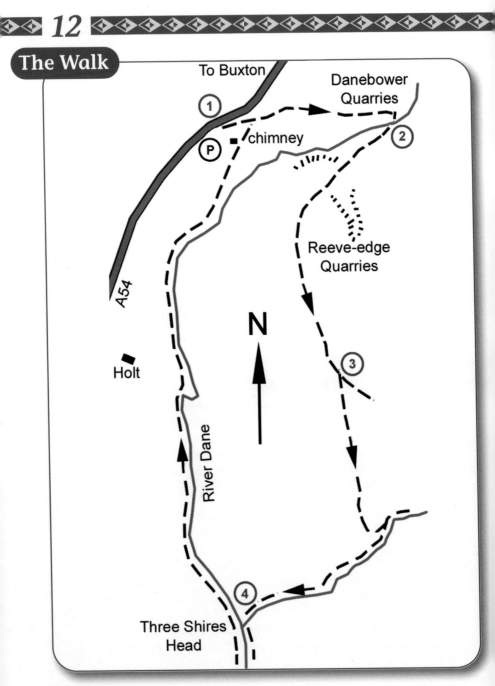

To Buxton

Danebower
Quarries

1

chimney

P

2

Reeve-edge
Quarries

A54

Holt

N

River Dane

3

4

Three Shires
Head

a ruined small, circular building that was once the Powder House. Try and imagine what it would have been like for the men who worked here.

2 Cross the infant River Dane on the helpful stones and scramble up the far side, then continue through the spoil heaps of Reeve-edge Quarries. You can explore the quarry, which hides out of sight to the left. Look across the valley – can you see your car? Now it is an easy walk along a level track with views across to the jagged outline of Ramshaw Rocks and The Roaches ahead.

A delightful spot for a photo opportunity.

3 About ¼ mile after the quarry, go through the gateway on the right and follow the path which leads down through an area of conical depressions or bell pits where coal was once mined. The obvious path keeps straight on, then curves left to descend to a rough track, where you go right. The track, in places worn down to the bedrock, leads past a pretty little packhorse bridge and continues down, above a steep, unfenced drop, to Three Shires Head.

4 The return route is over the larger gritstone bridge, where you move from Staffordshire into Derbyshire. Turn right and follow

the good path beside the River Dane gently upstream. Beyond a bridge cross the wooden stepstile and continue beside the Dane. The path then crosses the fields below Holt Farm – this bit can be boggy – before returning to the river along a recently flagged path, which passes a ruin.

Just below is the drainage level for the Dane Colliery. Beyond a little wooden gate look for the mountings of the colliery engine and the ruined flue. A race up to the chimney should speed the final ascent, then it's only a few more yards to the outward track.

◆ Background Notes ◆

Though the valley is now quiet and deserted, with only a scattering of farms, it was once a busy industrial area. The conical depressions in the field above Three Shires Head are the remains of **former coal mines**. Though usually such pits denote simple surface scrapings, the Blackclough Mine, whose entrance was at Burbage near Buxton, must have been a much grander affair, for it had boats on an underground canal.

Below Holt Farm a low archway can be seen beside the infant River Dane. This black tunnel disappearing into the earth is a drainage level for the **Dane Colliery**, which produced some of the best and cleanest coal in the Peak. The remarkably intact, tall **square-built chimney** standing on the hillside below the A54 is one of the relics of the colliery. Below the chimney a collapsed flue runs up the hillside and, at the foot, there are massive blocks of stone that once supported an engine.

The two disused gritstone quarries that flank the river are **Danebower** and **Reeve-edge**, which produced roofing slabs in the early 19th century.

The 'DVW' waymarks show the course of the **Dane Valley Way**, a 40-mile long-distance footpath, which leads beside the River Dane to its confluence with the River Wheelock at Middlewich.

Grin Low

Climb to the Tower

Enjoying a spot of map reading!

Perched on the top of Grin Low, high above Buxton, stands the gleaming white limestone tower of Solomon's Temple. It's in view from miles around, and the walk across the sheep-cropped turf to the summit is delightful. An ascent of the tower, set amid an alpine pasture, is a must, and a staircase spirals up within the folly to the turreted roof, where you look out over Buxton and the Peak District hills. This is a walk to encourage even the youngest to get out of the papoose carrier and give the adults a rest. Our youngest granddaughter, not yet two, climbed the steps to the top unaided, but, dwarfed by the parapet, children have to be lifted up to admire the view. So do your arm strengthening exercises the day before!

Kiddiwalks in the Peak District

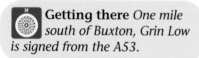 **Getting there** *One mile south of Buxton, Grin Low is signed from the A53.*

Length of walk 1 mile.
Time One to two hours.
Terrain Easy paths with a little ascent. Pushchair friendly if you don't mind lifting over the stiles.
Start/Parking Grin Low and Buxton Country Park picnic site off Grin Low Road, (toilets). Pay and display car park (GR 051719).
Map OS Explorer OL 24 – White Peak area.
Refreshments Take a picnic.

❶ Take the path from the far end of Grin Low car park, climbing past the quarry face. A couple of child-high signs show why you mustn't walk too near the cliffs. The path leads through a rocky cutting; then you turn right through the wooden kissing gate.

❷ You can't go wrong now, as Solomon's Temple is in view. Either follow the path down the steps and beside the wall, past a pond and a lime kiln, or choose your own route over the short cropped turf. An exciting spiral staircase, whose ascent needs supervision, climbs to the top of the tower, which has a high parapet and gives a splendid view over Buxton.

The Walk

To Grin Low Road and A54

N

P ①

②

④

③

Solomon's Temple

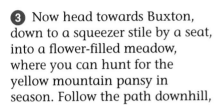

3 Now head towards Buxton, down to a squeezer stile by a seat, into a flower-filled meadow, where you can hunt for the yellow mountain pansy in season. Follow the path downhill, through old spoil heaps. The hollowed mound is called the 'frying pan', an old lime kiln with a 'handle' for the packhorses that brought the stone for burning.

Fun Things to See and Do ◆

Throughout the walk you will find information panels explaining the **history and wildlife of the park**. Out on the upland limestone grassland and in the wood keep a lookout for birds and hunt for the rare plants.

From the top of **Solomon's Temple** you can pick out Buxton's landmarks. Look for The Crescent, built by the Fifth Duke of Devonshire in the 1780s, and the huge dome of the Devonshire Royal Hospital, originally the Great Stables of the Duke of Devonshire. The exercise yard was covered with a dome, which was at that time the largest unsupported one in the world. Corbar Cross, high above the town, was erected in 1950 by local Roman Catholics, and in the distance you can see the steaming chimney of Hope Cement Works.

Also in Buxton Country Park, **Poole's Cavern**, the only entirely natural show cave in Derbyshire, is well worth a visit. It is named after an outlaw, Poole, who lived in the cave around 1440 and stashed away his loot in its gloomy depths. Ancient man also made his home in the cave, and it was later visited by the Romans, who were probably the first tourists! The cavern is famous for its stalactite and stalagmite formations, including the longest stalactite found in Derbyshire. The visitor centre has an exhibition, restaurant and shop. Open daily from February to November. Telephone: 01298 26978; www.poolescavern.co.uk

Buxton Go Ape, alongside Poole's Cavern, is a high wire forest adventure course for ages 10 plus. Open daily from March to October and weekends in November. Pre-booking essential: www.goape.co.uk; telephone 08456 439215

Kiddiwalks in the Peak District

13

4 Turn left over a stile by a five-bar gate into Grin Low Wood. Staying on the main track, the old packhorse way follows a level course across the hillside, while all around is evidence of lime burning. On reaching a T-junction, turn uphill. Then, just before you reach the wall, go right to Grin Quarry and back down through the cutting.

◆ Background Notes ◆

Solomon's Temple was built in 1896 by Solomon Mycock to provide work for unemployed quarrymen. It is on the site of a Neolithic tumulus, and excavations revealed six bodies and other remains, which are displayed in the visitor centre by Poole's Cavern.

The **'pudding pie' lime kilns** date from the mid 17th century. These were dome shaped and built out of rock and earth, with a hole at the top. Layers of limestone, coal and wood were built up and set alight from a hole in the bottom.

The 100-acre **Grin Low Wood** was planted around 1820 by the 6th Duke of Devonshire to hide from the inhabitants the scars of quarrying and lime burning, described by James Croston: 'There is not a vestige of green to be seen upon the parched surface, vegetation being entirely precluded by the sulphurous fumes which arise from the smelting furnaces. Havoc and destruction are everywhere apparent, the bowels of the mountain seem literally torn out and the rocky ruin spread before the eye excites in the mind the idea of nature returned again to universal chaos.' By the end of the 18th century the whole area was covered in a million tons of waste, and the lime burners even made their homes in caves hollowed in the solidified spoil heaps. The level open areas are the remains of these waste ash tips. Yet now Grin Low has flowers as fine as anywhere in the Peak District. The grass of Parnassus, autumn gentian, devil's bit scabious, common spotted orchids and the tall purple spears of the fragrant orchid can all be seen here in abundance. We even found the rare frog orchid.

Limestone was extracted from **Grin Quarry** until 1972, but now kestrels nest on the cliffs and the quarry hides a caravan park.

14

Deep Dale and Taddington

A Flowery Walk

Setting off towards Taddington.

Ever wondered what a million looks like? Well in spring you can get an idea from the cowslips in Deep Dale, for at that time of year the sides of the valley are thick with their nodding golden blooms. There must be more cowslips here than anywhere else in the Peak District. But first there's the climb towards Taddington (the longer walk takes you all the way there). If you're considering moving house then this is the place to be. It might be the fresh air or the hard work, but in the 17th century the inhabitants of this village were famous for living a long time. As one old lady put it, 'folk did no die there young'. Certainly young or old it's a delightful spot, reached along packhorse ways and old miners' tracks, with frequent stops to look at the sheep and cows. The Queen's Arms provides a welcome break but, for young ones, the highlight of the day could be the village's slide and swings.

Kiddiwalks in the Peak District

14

Getting there *The starting point is 7 miles east of Buxton, on the A6.*

Length of walk 3½ miles (or 5 miles if you include Taddington).
Time Allow 3 (or 5) hours.
Terrain A steady climb on easy paths, then a steep descent to a flowery dale.

Start/Parking White Lodge picnic site on the A6, pay and display car park, toilets (GR 170706).
Map Explorer OL 24 – White Peak area.
Refreshments Take a picnic, or, on the longer walk, visit the Queen's Arms, Taddington, which has picnic tables in the car park.

◆ Fun Things to See and Do ◆

The glory of the White Peak dales is the **flowers**. Deep Dale is at its best when smothered with cowslips, but there are lots of other flowers for the children to see and identify. Look for the flower spikes of the early purple orchid and the rare mountain pansy. You don't have to hunt for them, just watch where you are putting your feet! A flower book is a must on this walk.

Look for **relics of lead mining** and see what sort of flowers bloom on the old spoil heaps. Why are the spoil heaps often bare of flowers? It's because most flowers don't like the lead that remains in the soil. Spring sandwort, also called leadwort, is one that can tolerate these conditions. Lead is very dangerous for animals and so that's why lead rakes are usually fenced.

Most of the paths are waymarked, so the children will enjoy looking out for the next arrow.

The longer walk visits **Taddington**, where you can look for the old mile post. There is also a children's playground, which our grandchildren thought the best bit of the walk.

Deep Dale and Taddington

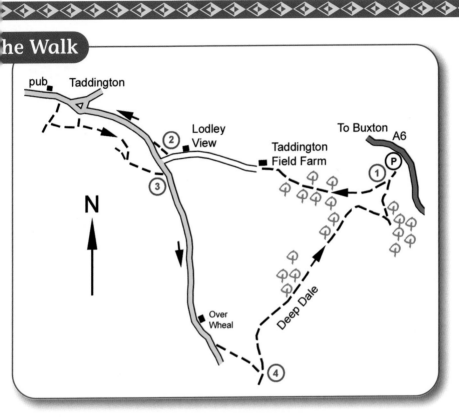

❶ A good path sets off from the side of White Lodge car park. Beyond a kissing gate look for a waymarked post, signed 'Taddington', that points you up the grassy hillside where every mossy rock is dotted with tiny flowers in season. Entering the woodland, you climb on up the steep-sided Dimon Dale through coppiced hazel trees, which were frequently cut down to produce timber for lead mining. There's a short, rough bit of path; then you continue through the field until a wooden sign points to a small gate by Taddington Field Farm. Now follow the farm lane past Lodley View Farm and keep straight on.

❷ When the road starts to go downhill the *longer walk* forks right down the narrow track, but the *shorter walk* continues to the T-junction and turns left, continuing from point 3. The *longer walk* joins the tarmac lane known as The Gates, where you keep straight on into Taddington.

14

Immediately beyond the Bramwell Memorial Institute the route turns left up the hill, but first you can explore the village and call in at the Queen's Arms. Dokindale Road, an old green lane, climbs past the playground and about 150 yards beyond this a wooden footpath sign points left. The grassy track curves across the hillside to meet another track where you turn right. Now the walled lane climbs gently to meet another track where you keep left to join a metalled lane where, reunited with the *shorter walk*, you turn right.

❸ Both routes now continue along the tarmac lane, with a wide view left over Monsal Dale

to the flat-topped Fin Cop. You go by the humpy ground of an ancient lead rake (a hillock left by mining along a mineral vein); then, about 100 yards after passing Over Wheal Farm, a signpost marks a footpath on the left. This crosses the field diagonally to a squeezer stile and slants down through scattered hawthorns into Deep Dale – aim for the bottom of the path visible opposite.

4 Joining the valley path by a stile, turn left. Then, at a little gate, the path continues on the other side of the wall. This is a typical dry limestone dale covered in vast drifts of cowslips during early May. The bridleway heads down the broad grassy valley floor past lead workings where a metal cylinder on the far side of the wall covers a deep shaft on the Town Head vein. After climbing past a little rocky bluff you continue down the dale until an arrow points left, down between the limestone cliffs. Then you cross a stile and scramble by the stream to join the good path back to White Lodge car park.

Background Notes ◆

Lead is found in rakes, which may be many feet wide and extend for several miles, and was mined by the Romans in the first and second centuries AD. Mining was revived by the time of the Domesday Book and continued through medieval times, and by the 17th and early 18th centuries there was a flourishing industry in the Peak District. Wheal is an old Cornish word for mine, so men from Cornwall must have worked at Over Wheal Farm.

Taddington, at over 1,000 ft, is one of the highest villages in Derbyshire. The name comes from a Saxon chief called Tada who settled here after the Romans left. Though quiet enough today, as it is bypassed by the busy A6, a cast iron mile post shows that from 1812 the Main Street was once the main turnpike route to London. There is the Queen's Arms pub and a restored 14th-century church, whose Saxon cross is possibly the oldest in Derbyshire.

15

Chatsworth

Waterworks in the Wood

The highlight of this walk must be the cannons. Pointing out over the Derwent Valley from beside the Elizabethan Hunting Tower, high in the woods above Chatsworth, their barrels are polished smooth with the attentions of countless children. But before you get to them there's the walk up through the trees, where a rustle in the undergrowth causes even grown-up imaginations to dwell on thoughts of a wolf or a bear. And it's not just an uphill plod, for there's a secret staircase through the rocks and a waterfall from whose top you look almost straight down on Chatsworth's garden below. Even the descent is fun, with a long stone staircase curving down through the trees and a handrail to provide reassurance for the children as well as grandpa carrying the youngest in a papoose carrier. Note: Chatsworth Park and Stand Wood are open all year.

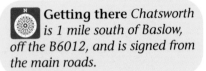

Getting there *Chatsworth is 1 mile south of Baslow, off the B6012, and is signed from the main roads.*

Length of walk 1 mile.
Time One to two hours.
Terrain A steep ascent and descent with lots of steps. Not suitable for pushchairs, but there are lots of level walks along the numerous paths in the park.
Start/Parking Chatsworth House. Car park charge, toilets (GR 261703). Between Christmas and mid March the car park is closed; so park about a mile away near Calton Lees (GR 259686), from where a path follows the river.
Map OS Explorer OL 24 – White Peak area.
Refreshments Chatsworth House, except between Christmas and mid March.

1 From Chatsworth House follow the tarmac track past the 18th-century stable block and over the cattle grid – fun to balance across. Fork right to the 'Stand Wood Walks', just before the entrance to the adventure playground and farmyard, and follow the tarmac track uphill.

Fun Things to See and Do ◆

Climbing up and down steps high above Chatsworth House makes for **an adventurous walk**. Woodland is always good for hide and seek, but the paths are so convoluted perhaps it's best to leave the hiding until after the ascent. We can't afford to lose any readers! The children also love swinging on the trees and jumping off logs.

The **Souter Stone** is a good place to explain how the fountain works – the water comes from up here, so tell the story of how the Sixth Duke built a fountain, just to impress the Tsar, it's a true life fairy tale.

To visit just **Chatsworth House and Gardens** makes a full day out, but in addition there's the **farmyard**, with animal handling and many activities and demonstrations, and also a huge **woodland adventure playground**.

Kiddiwalks in the Peak District

15

On reaching a stone barn, turn left into the trees.

2 The path crosses a track; then you fork right by the large Brownhill Oak Tree and continue through the trees to The Dell, a meeting of the ways. Continuing up the steps, the path crosses a tarmac track, then leads through woodland and goes under the tall pillars of the aqueduct, where water pours off the end. Follow the path uphill, past the beginning of the aqueduct, then continue up the steps and head left. The path continues across the hillside. Turn right at a junction up more steps through a rocky cutting, complete with chain

handrail. On reaching a higher path, turn right to a waterfall and climb more steps to the top of the Souter Stone, to a lovely pool with a splendid view down into the gardens.

3 Now turn left along the broad Lower Emperor Track through the mixed woodland. Here you can look out for bracket fungus, and soon you pass an enormous beech tree, which is really good to climb on. Briefly join a tarmac track; then take the path on the left to the Hunting Tower. Children love sitting on the cannons and there is a splendid view. Can you see Edensor village and the church?

The Walk

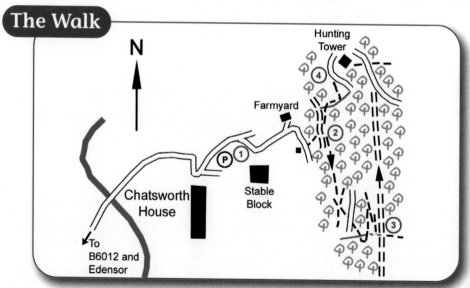

4 A path descends steps to a tarmac track, where you go left and then almost immediately right, down more steps. The path continues through the trees, then plunges down a very long, steep flight of steps, which fortunately has a chain handrail. At the bottom you cross a stream, then the path leads back to Brownhill Oak Tree, where you follow your outward route back across the track to the tarmac track and the adventure playground.

Background Notes ◆

The present Chatsworth is basically the creation of **the First Duke** who between 1686 and 1707 almost entirely rebuilt the house and also added the formal gardens, including the tumbling waters of the cascade, though the huge waterspout of the Emperor Fountain came much later.

The slopes to the east of Chatsworth were, until the 18th century, bare and rocky. When the Chatsworth estate was landscaped around 1760, by Capability Brown, **Stand Wood** was planted with beech, sycamore, Spanish chestnut and a few conifers. In the 19th century more conifers were added and an undershrub of *Rhododendron ponticum*, while other species of trees colonised the woodland naturally.

The walks in Stand Wood were laid out between 1835 and 1845 by Joseph Paxton under the direction of the Sixth Duke of Devonshire. The Duke was expecting the **Tsar of Russia** to stay at Chatsworth in 1844, so he commissioned Paxton to build him the Emperor Fountain, to be bigger and better than one he had seen in Russia. A 2½-mile conduit was dug to supply the Emperor Lake, high above the house, which is topped up by Swiss Lake. Hidden in the wood you will find the lakes, waterfalls and aqueducts that supply the jet. Alas the Tsar never came, but the fountain, which rises a staggering 290 ft into the air, is still there to delight Chatsworth's modern-day visitors.

The Elizabethan **Hunting Tower** stands rather aloof from the grand house, up in Stand Wood. It was built about 1582 by Bess of Hardwick so that she could watch the hounds. The iron cannons on the forecourt came from a ship which fought at the Battle of Trafalgar.

73

16

Lathkill Dale

Underground Wealth

With vertical limestone cliffs towering overhead, and slopes covered in harebells, thyme, hawkbit and rock-roses, Lathkill Dale is a summer's delight. But hidden in the undergrowth, ready for exploring children to find, are the remains of a very different past. Beside the path a wire cage tops an ancient mineshaft, while tempting short tunnels hint at the past when every rocky cleft was explored in the search for minerals, but best of all there's a house with the biggest and scariest cellar in the world. It's not clear why Mr Bateman built his house on top of a mineshaft, but he did, and his wife, a forgiving sort, got on with the housework as usual until one day her broom went clean through the floor. Suddenly she was looking straight down the shaft. It's not recorded what she said, but you can climb down a ladder beside the ruins and peer into the black depths of the mine.

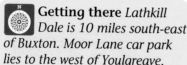 **Getting there** *Lathkill Dale is 10 miles south-east of Buxton. Moor Lane car park lies to the west of Youlgreave.*

Length of walk 5 miles.
Time About 5 hours.
Terrain Good paths all the way.
NB: The limestone steps are very slippery when wet.
Start/Parking Moor Lane pay and display car park and picnic area (GR 194645).
Map OS Explorer OL 24 – White Peak area.

Refreshments Pack a picnic – or there are pubs and cafés at nearby Monyash.

1 Turn left out of Moor Lane car park; then, at the road junction, take the footpath opposite. A clear path crosses the fields to Low Moor Wood, a 50th Anniversary Woodland of the Peak National Park, originally planted in the 1800s. Continue over the fields and walk through the trees behind Calling Low Farm. Then, with a bird's-eye

◆ Fun Things to See and Do ◆

 The children had fun **counting sheep** in the fields, **climbing stone stepstiles**, and **hunting for fossils** in the long flight of steps.

The ruins of **Bateman's house** are great to explore. Try and identify the rooms from the plan, while braver members of the party will want to descend the precipitous ladder into Lathkill's underworld.

Visit the **Mandale Mine's Engine House** where steps behind the ruin lead up to an information board and the old mine entrance. We've been inside, but now it's fenced off in the name of Health and Safety. The Mandale Sough, which drained the mine, runs beside by the track.

Just before the **Water Bailiff's House** look for the notice that proclaims 'This footpath is open to visitors except Thursday in Easter week. Toll on that day 1 penny each person'.

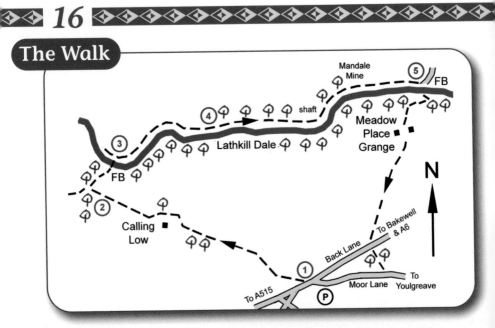

view of Lathkill Dale, head down over the fields.

2 In the nature reserve, a long flight of limestone steps descends steeply into Cales Dale. How many steps are there? When you reach the bottom, turn right through the trees and follow the path down into Lathkill Dale.

3 Cross the footbridge and turn right. The path leads down the dale beside the River Lathkill. Beyond a stone stepstile you pass Pudding Springs, a pretty waterfall made of tufa, a naturally porous deposit of calcium carbonate found only in very pure limestone streams. At

Cow Gate pool, the header pool for the leats supplying the waterwheels of the Lathkill Dale mines, look out for two huge abandoned millstones by the path, all that remains of Carter's Mill, an early 19th-century corn mill.

4 The path now enters Palmerston Wood. Look for the capped shaft of the Lathkill mine, which in 1836 had a huge waterwheel, 'the second largest in the kingdom'. The track now divides and it is prone to flooding – which path is the quickest? A wooden bridge leads to Bateman's house, whose shaft is a must. Then you pass the ruined stone piers of the aqueduct. Just before you leave the wood look for a little path on the left, which leads up to the ruined Mandale engine house. The main path continues beneath a flowery bank and you pass two trial levels, safe for children to explore.

5 At whitewashed Lathkill Lodge, the water bailiff's house, cross the clapper bridge and follow the broad path which zigzags up through a bluebell wood. Turning left on gaining the field, you then head for Meadow Place Grange. Cross the spacious courtyard to a high stone stile, then follow the rightmost wall to a signpost where an obvious path crosses the fields. Going straight over Back Lane, the field path crosses a belt of woodland concealing the chasm of Long

At the Mandale engine house.

Rake, an old lead mine. Finally, on reaching quiet Moor Lane, walk back up to the car park.

Kiddiwalks in the Peak District

 *16*

◆ Background Notes ◆

At the bottom of **Cales Dale**, by the footbridge over the River Lathkill, are stone walls partly obscured by vegetation. These are the remains of a medieval sheepwash built by the monks of One Ash Grange, the farm on the plateau high above.

The **Mandale mine** is one of the oldest mines in Derbyshire and is thought to have been worked since Roman times. It was always prone to flooding and so tunnels or soughs were dug to try and drain the water. In 1798 the Mandale Mine Company started to drive the Mandale sough, which took an incredible thirty years to complete, and the exit, beside the River Lathkill, is still in good repair. As the sough proved inadequate, a 35-ft diameter waterwheel was added in 1840 and the water to drive the pump was supplied by a leat that crossed high above the river, along an aqueduct whose truncated stone pillars still stand. In 1848 a Cornish beam engine was installed to improve the drainage, but it was still insufficient and the mine closed in 1851.

Meadow Place Grange has buildings set round a courtyard and retains the original plan of the medieval monastic grange. This stone-built farm belonged to Leicester Abbey from the 12th century until the dissolution of the monasteries by Henry VIII in the 16th century. From the large irregular meadows above the farm there are wide views across the dale to the contrasting narrow strip fields on the far side.

Stanton Moor

Rocky Tors and a Stone Circle

The path on Stanton Moor.

Getting turned to stone is not a common hazard these days, but the stones of Stanton Moor stone circle are said to be the petrified remains of nine maidens who unwisely chose to perform a pagan dance here on the Sabbath. The Cork Stone, though, is natural and the ascent, using its iron rings and footholds, is a must. Surrounded by White Peak limestone this is a geological island, and scattered across the gritstone moor are cairns and over seventy burial mounds dating back to the Bronze Age. Set amid a sea of heather and gorse the moor is at its best in late summer, ablaze in gold and purple. Of all the stone circles in the Peak District this is one of the finest and certainly the best known. So while the children should certainly be encouraged to dance, why not just relax on the honey scented heather or collect some finger-staining bilberries?

Kiddiwalks in the Peak District

17

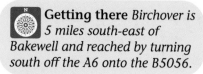 **Getting there** *Birchover is 5 miles south-east of Bakewell and reached by turning south off the A6 onto the B5056.*

Length of walk 2½ miles.
Time About 2 hours.
Terrain An easy walk on rough little paths.
Start/Parking Birchover Road, between Birchover and Stanton in Peak. There is a free car park opposite Birchover Stone Ltd, south of the starting point, and limited roadside parking at the start of the walk (GR 242625).
Map OS Explorer OL 24 – White Peak area.
Refreshments Take a picnic or visit the Druid Inn at Birchover.

1 A footpath, 250 yards along Birchover Road from the car park, leads through the trees onto

◆ Fun Things to See and Do ◆

 Before you set off tell the children the story of the **Nine Ladies stone circle**. Built four thousand years ago, the circle has a small king stone, said to be the petrified figure of the fiddler, which indicates the stones may have had an astronomical function.

The **Cork Stone** just asks to be climbed, but probably only by the adults and older children. A safer challenge is the **OS trig point**, especially if posing for a photo.

Don't miss nearby **Birchover**, a pretty little village of gritstone houses, with a couple of pubs, a village shop and a pinfold, but its most interesting feature is well concealed. Hidden behind the Druid Inn is a fascinating warren of hollowed out gritstone blocks known as **Rowter Rocks** or the **Druid Stones**. For children, and most adults too, this is a fascinating place to explore. At one time the stones were thought to have been the work of the ancients, hence the name of Druid Stones, but it was all done by one man. Working entirely by himself, Thomas Eyre, the local vicar, carved from the solid rock a magnificent series of caves, tunnels and stairways. Right on the top, there is even a stone chair from which to admire the view across the valley towards the River Wye.

The Walk

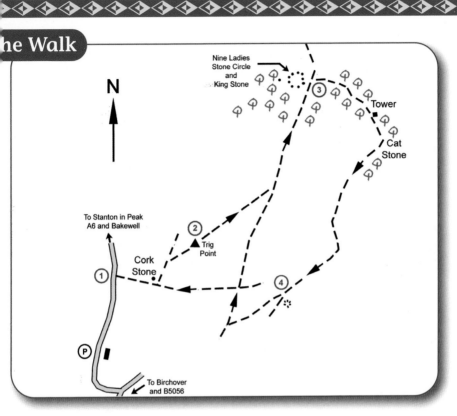

Stanton Moor. Beyond the 'Life and Death' notice board you reach the Cork Stone, ascent of which is harder than it looks. Here you turn left; then, passing the old quarry, fork right and take the path which climbs through heather to the OS trig point.

2 Now a narrow path, just one child wide, leads gently downhill through more heather. Joining a broad track, turn left and continue through the trees to Nine Ladies stone circle. The children can count the stones and look for the king stone.

3 Returning to the track, by the spooky notice board, take the path straight ahead, which leads through scattered woodland to a stile by the Earl Grey Tower. Turning right, you follow the path beside the fence above a steep wooded slope with extensive views across the Derwent Valley. At the bend in the fence the children can look for the date on the Cat Stone. The path now goes above a deep quarry (out of sight, but there's a warning sign) and continues to a bend in the fence where there is a viewpoint on a rocky outcrop.

4 Cross the stile to the 'Tracks Through Time' notice board and continue down to join a major track. Here you turn right and climb to a crossroads by the largest tumulus on the moor, which contained 13 burials. Finally you turn left, back to the Cork Stone.

◆ Background Notes ◆

The **burial mounds** scattered on Stanton Moor were all excavated between 1927 and 1950 by J. and J.P. Heathcote who established a private museum at Birchover. It was a very special place for our ancestors who built these ceremonial monuments to their dead 4,000 years ago.

The **Cork Stone**, with its eroded carved footholds and iron rungs set into the rock, presents an obvious challenge. The inscription 'WWM 1864', hidden under the overhang, is possibly the initials of the quarryman who carried out the work, and the nearby quarry is a good sheltered picnic spot. In the 18th century this isolated boulder was surrounded by four standing stones.

The **Earl Grey Tower**, standing on the edge of Stanton Moor, was built in 1832 to commemorate that landmark in democracy, the passing of the Reform Bill.

The **Cat Stone** is an isolated gritstone tor whose carved footholds and inscription 'EIN 1831' were the work of the Thornhill family of Stanton Hall.

8

Manifold Valley

A Disappearing River and a Huge Cave

Thor's Cave seen from the Manifold Valley.

C ave of the Thunder God! What child, or adult too, could resist this for a walk? Towering high over the Manifold Valley rises a vertical, gleaming wall of limestone rock and centre stage is the vast gaping mouth of Thor's Cave. Fully sixty feet high, this is one of the biggest cave entrances in England. Polished rocks, worn smooth by generations of explorers, make even getting inside an adventure, usually more feared by adults than children. When you've scrabbled up, there are dark corners to explore (take a torch) and an echo – try shouting! Then afterwards there's paddling in the River Manifold at Wettonmill, before cakes and ice cream at the tearoom.

Kiddiwalks in the Peak District

18

 Getting there *Wettonmill car park is 10 miles south of Buxton.*

Length of walk 3½ miles.
Time About 3 hours.
Terrain A steep climb up grassy slopes, then lots of steps on the descent. **NB:** Limestone can be very slippery when wet. The tarmac track along the Manifold Valley is an excellent excursion in its own right for pushchairs (see map).

Start/Parking Wettonmill car park (GR 095561), which has toilets.
Map OS Explorer OL 24 – White Peak area.
Refreshments Wetton's Royal Oak has a family room and beer garden, while the home-made cakes at Wettonmill Tearoom are delicious.

1 Cross the four-arched bridge, built in 1807 by the Duke of Devonshire, to the tearoom. Ignore for the moment its

◆ Fun Things to See and Do ◆

 The highlight of the walk is **Thor's Cave**, and a scramble inside – very slippery if wet – yields the finest view, with the hillside framed in a black silhouette. There is even a window, a narrow slot high on the right. Visit **Buxton Museum** to see some of the artefacts that were found here.

From the footpath just above Wettonmill you can also visit **Nan Tor Cave**. Like Thor's Cave this was formed by an underground stream. It is fun to explore and the river here is a good paddling spot.

Lots of special **lime-loving flowers** grow in the Manifold Valley and the limestone itself is full of the fossil remains of shellfish and corals.

From the **highest point on the walk** you look down on a barn that collects rainwater from the roof. Why are there no pools up here and why are the side valleys dry?

The Walk

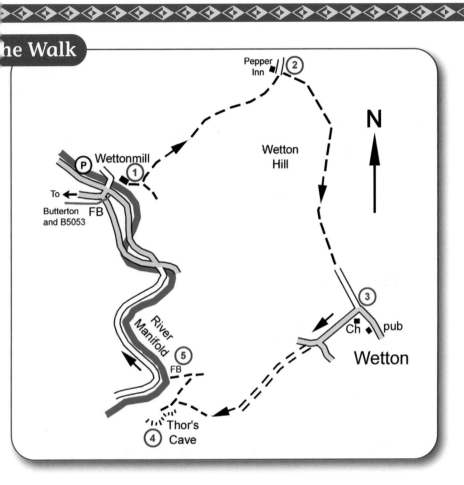

beguiling welcome. A footpath sign points between the buildings and the path leads along the field edge and up the hillside. At the top a waymark points left, and the path heads down to a wooden gate where you keep straight on, up the dry grassy dale. On either side are very steep slopes with parallel ridges caused by the earth slipping downhill.

2 Reaching the old manor house, known as Pepper Inn, which was once a button factory and also an isolation hospital during a smallpox outbreak among the workmen building the Manifold Railway, you turn right through a squeezer stile. Cross a little clapper bridge. The path follows the drystone wall steeply uphill to a stile; continuing across a field. You then climb to the highest point on the walk, where the view stretches across the Manifold Valley to Grindon church. Crossing a squeezer stile, now head down the tarmac track into Wetton.

❸ The Royal Oak is just a few yards further, but our route turns right. Walk along the lane to the road junction, turn right and then go left down the track signed 'Concession Path to Thor's Cave'. At the track end a waymark points over a stone stepstile and the path follows the wall down, dipping across a valley to a little wooden gate, and then descends to Thor's Cave.

❹ From the massive entrance there is a bird's-eye view of the Manifold Valley. After you have explored the gloomy depths of the cave, follow the stepped path down through the trees. This crosses the hillside to join another path, which leads down to a footbridge over the River Manifold. Don't miss the information board.

❺ Now turn right along the tarmac track past the huge bulk

of Ossoms Crag, a very impressive piece of rock architecture, and cross a wooden bridge; then take the left branch of the road which leads below Darfar Crags. The small cave high in the limestone wall is known as the 'Hermit's Cave', but the hermit must have been a good climber, as the route is graded 'very severe'. Follow the road over Dafar Bridge; then splash across the ford, or use the footbridge. You are then back at Wettonmill, which was once a railway station, while the car park stands on top of the old Botstone Lead Mine, which had an 18 ft diameter waterwheel.

◆ Background Notes ◆

In all but the wettest conditions the **River Manifold** disappears below Wettonmill and does not appear again until it wells up in the grounds of Ilam Hall (see Walk 20).

Wettonmill dates from the end of the 16th century and was originally a corn mill. It closed in the middle of the 19th century and now does a roaring trade selling refreshments.

Palaeolithic hunters lived under the great roof of **Thor's Cave** and watched wolves, bears and woolly rhinoceros in the valley below. In 1864 the cave was excavated by a Wetton schoolmaster, Samuel Carrington, who found Romano-British remains of pottery, and bronze and iron knives, which are in Buxton Museum.

Wetton dates back to the 7th century. Old stone cottages cluster round the Royal Oak pub, the Reading Room and the sturdy church, which has an ancient tower.

The tarmac track down the valley was the course of the **Leek & Manifold Valley Light Railway**, one of the least successful enterprises of the railway era. As was said at the time, 'It starts in the middle of nowhere and ends up in the same place'. The track was converted to its present use as a footpath by Staffordshire Council as long ago as 1937.

Dove Dale

Stepping Stones and a Mini Mountain

Negotiating the stepping stones.

R ising steeply above Dove Dale the truncated pyramid of Thorpe Cloud is an irresistible challenge to anyone who loves hills. The climb doesn't look much from the river, though it's five hundred feet of steep ascent straight up to the summit, and when you get to the top you meet the nicest people. 'Do you mind if we borrow your children?' we asked and the four girls obligingly posed on this summit. Yet this ancient coral reef knoll, polished to a smooth gloss by thousands of visitors, isn't a hill at all, merely the remains of the expansive plateau of the White Peak, into which the River Dove has cut. From the summit, with a bird's-eye view of the valley far below, you can feel justly superior to the folk who only made it as far as the stepping stones, but try and chose a quiet time for your visit, for on a sunny bank holiday the valley can look more like Blackpool beach.

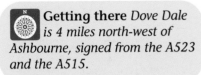

Getting there *Dove Dale is 4 miles north-west of Ashbourne, signed from the A523 and the A515.*

Length of walk 1½ miles.
Time About 2 hours.
Terrain An adventurous little walk. The climb up Thorpe Cloud is definitely not suitable for pushchairs, but there's a tarmac track from the car park to the stepping stones. **NB:** Take care of venturesome children on the summit of Thorpe Cloud, which has unfenced cliffs.
Start/Parking Follow signs to Dove Dale from nearby roads and

head to Dove Dale car park (GR 146509). Charge, toilets.
Map OS Explorer OL 24 – White Peak area.
Refreshments There is a refreshment hut in Dove Dale car park and usually an ice cream van by the stepping stones in the summer months.

❶ From Dove Dale car park entrance turn right and walk beside the River Dove, past the 1969 Isaac Walton Gauging Station, which measures the river flow. Cross the wooden footbridge, and, heading away from the river, keep straight on beside the fence, climbing gently round the

The Walk

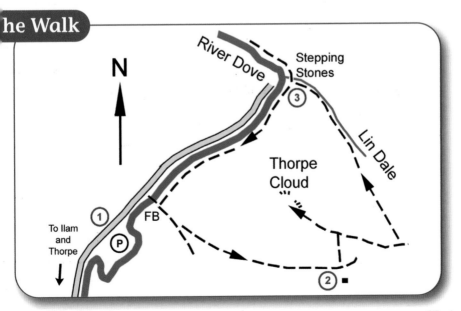

Kiddiwalks in the Peak District

lower flanks of Thorpe Cloud. Forking left, continue climbing across the grassy hillslope to a small barn.

2 Now head left up steep, pathless grass to join the obvious path which leads up the ridge to the knobbly crest. Take care above the dizzy drops at the far end, where you get a bird's-eye view of Dove Dale and across the valley to Bunster Hill. There is a popular path, which goes straight down to the stepping stones, but it is very steep and you will find it much easier to return by the ridge path. Stay on the path, which heads to the left of the barn to

◆ Fun Things to See and Do ◆

The ascent of **Thorpe Cloud** is a splendid expedition for small children, as you really feel you have climbed a mountain. How many people can you see on the top? The name Cloud means hill, while Thorpe is the nearby village. Children can hunt for fossil shells on the summit rocks.

The **stepping stones** are great fun to cross, and it's a splendid, safe paddling spot, but you don't have to negotiate the stones, as there is a path on both sides of the Dove back to the car park.

You may see **dippers** by the riverside. These are small dark brown birds with white bibs, which bob up and down as they sit on the rocks looking for fish. You can also look for **trout** in any deep pools.

meet the wall, then curves left. After about 200 yards a broad, grassy path leads down Lin Dale, where, in August, pretty blood-drop emlets, a golden flower with large red spots, grow in the boggy valley bottom.

3 Either cross the stepping stones to the tarmac track or stay beneath the slopes of Thorpe Cloud and follow the riverside path downstream to the footbridge.

Background Notes ◆

Although born on the gritstone moorlands of the Dark Peak, the **Dove** runs for much of its course on limestone, and rivers on limestone have the habit of disappearing down cracks and fissures into a subterranean world. The Dove is different. Despite all the rules it stays obstinately above ground. The reason is chiefly because the bed is waterproofed by clay. But why does it meander so? Rivers meander when they flow on the plains, but here it is in a steep sided gorge. All becomes clear when you stand on the summit and look at the surrounding hills. They are all at the same level; this was once a plain into which the rivers and streams incised their valleys. When the land was lifted up in the massive earth movements of mid Pliocene times, the river continued to cut its way down, but its course was already set in the form of its early years.

More than a million people visit Dove Dale each year and the famous **Dovedale stepping stones** are as popular as ever – it has been estimated that at peak times as many as 3,000 visitors per hour stagger or stride across!

The nearby **Izaak Walton Hotel** is named after the author who wrote *The Compleat Angler*, the famous fishing classic published in 1653.

Blood-drop emlets, *Mimulus luteus*, are a species of monkey flower, a garden escape introduced here from South America. They like boggy places, and with a bit of imagination the flower can be seen to resemble a grinning face.

20

Ilam

A Hermit and a Boiling River

S treams in limestone country have the habit of disappearing either suddenly into chasms, or leaking away into a subterranean underground. The River Manifold is one of the latter, as below Wettonmill (see Walk 18) it vanishes through innumerable fissures in its bed. But, after a long and mysterious journey through the underworld, out comes the river into daylight at Ilam Hall, churning like a boiling kettle. Once ladies in flowing dresses paraded sedately below the hall and eminent figures like Samuel Johnson came to stay. But it's no accident that Ilam village looks like a set for *The Sound of Music*, for the owner of the hall loved the Alps and remodelled the village in the Swiss style. We've got the children, all we need now is Julie Andrews!

Getting there *Ilam village is 4 miles north-west of Ashbourne, signed from the A523 and A52.*

Length of walk 1 mile.
Time Allow 1 hour.
Terrain Easy walk over short grass and then a surfaced path. The steps can be avoided if you have a pushchair.
Start/Parking Ilam Park NT pay and display (members free) car park (GR 132507), toilets. More information available from

www.nationaltrust.org.uk or telephone: 01335 350503.
Map Explorer OL 24 – White Peak area.
Refreshments Manifold Tearoom (NT) – open at weekends throughout the year and every day in July and August; see website for other days of opening.

1 A sign from the left rear corner of the car park says 'Pedestrians this way'. Follow this path for about 50 yards; then go sharp right through the large

he Walk

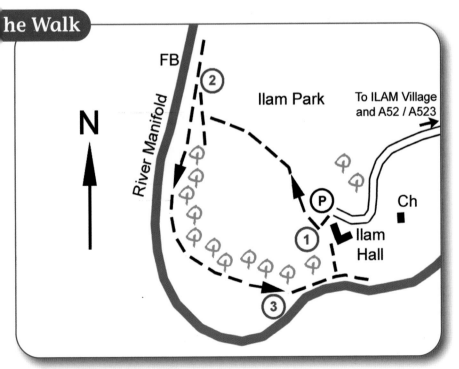

Kiddiwalks in the Peak District

wrought iron gate. A track curves across the short grass of the parkland, but you can choose your own route. Head for the fenced pond and a clump of trees; then, at the lowest point, join a bumpy track that leads down into the valley.

◆ Fun Things to See and Do ◆

The most interesting feature on this walk is **the river**. After looking at the dry bed the children can see the water reappearing at the **Boil Hole**.

All children, and most grown-ups, will enjoy exploring the turret and parapet of the **Italian gardens**, which were built about 1830. The plant containers came from the old hall, what do you think they used to be?

Look for the **Russell coat of arms** over the main entrance to Ilam Hall and hunt for a **carved table and stool** on the sloping paths above the Boil Hole.

There are many links at Ilam with **St Bertram**, a Mercian prince whose family was killed by wolves. Imagine what it would be like to live in the small cave by the Boil Hole. You can visit his bridge, his well, and the church, which has his chapel. Medieval pilgrims came to visit his tomb and miracle cures were claimed by those who crawled through the holes in the covering.

The **visitor centre**, which tells you all about the park and the hall, has a relief map of the area with buttons to press and family and children's guides. Check before your visit that the shop and tearoom are open, or that promised ice cream may be a disappointment.

In nice weather the **grassy slopes and banks by the river** are a great place to picnic, play games or just laze around.

2 The route goes left, but first detour right to visit the long, narrow footbridge over the River Manifold, most of which has vanished underground, so it is often dry in the summer months. Now follow the path below the wooded hillslope, which in spring is smothered with white flowered ramsons. What do you think this was once used for? Crush a leaf and you will find it smells strongly of garlic. You pass the Battle Cross, which was found in the foundations of a cottage. How did it get its name? This is Paradise Walk, which was created as an informal promenade for the residents of Ilam Hall. The low stone walls are good for balancing along.

At Ilam Hall.

3 Next you return to the river, which magically is now full of water, and pass a small cave and the Boil Hole, where the river bubbles up after its underground journey. Ahead

you can see St Bertram's Bridge, the original road bridge. Now turn left and climb the steps. These lead to the bottom of the tower, where a spiral staircase goes up to the Italian gardens, visitor centre, shop and tearoom.

◆ Background Notes ◆

The original **Ilam Hall** was built in the 1820s in the Tudor Gothic style by Jesse Watts-Russell, a London businessman, on the site of an earlier 16th-century dwelling and included towers, turrets and twisted chimneys. He removed those houses too close to his new mansion and went on to demolish the rest of the village before rebuilding it in the alpine style, with steep gables and ornate bargeboards. The old road to Blore passed uncomfortably close to the hall, so it was realigned and is now at the other end of the village. The hall, however, stood for barely a hundred years, but when they started to demolish it, and after about three-quarters of the building had gone, it was purchased by Sir Robert McDougall, the well known name in flour. After making the remaining portion safe, he gave it, together with the grounds, to the National Trust on the understanding that it was to be used as a Youth Hostel.

In **Ilam** itself the half-timbered building that resembles a church is the village school, built in 1854, and the adjacent house was for the schoolmaster. The large Victorian Gothic cross was erected by Mr Watts-Russell in memory of his wife Mary and he also had a go at improving Ilam church by adding an octagonal mausoleum.

The **River Manifold** disappears because its bed is seamed with innumerable fissures and in all but the wettest conditions the river sinks into the underworld.

Tradition says that **St Bertram** once lived in prayer and meditation in the small cave where the River Manifold emerges into daylight. However, having a hermit living in a cave was a popular foible of Victorian gentry, who paid the incumbent a small fee.